MW00609713

The Future of Sales Compensation

Chad Albrecht

Steve Marley

ZS Associates, Inc.

Published by ZS Associates, Inc.
1800 Sherman Avenue, Suite 700
Evanston, Illinois 60201

www.zsassociates.com

Text design: Ganesh Singh

Typesetting and project management: Books By Design, Inc.

Library of Congress Control Number: 2016930337

ISBN: 978-0-9853436-5-1

Contents

Foreword

By Andris A. Zoltners
Founding Director, ZS

The Impact of Sales Incentive Compensation

At least three-quarters of companies will change their sales incentive compensation plan this year. That's a lot of companies that are not just changing their quotas—many are making structural modifications to their plans. Companies change sales incentive plans for many reasons. Some want to better align incentives with new strategies, such as entering new markets or launching products. Some seek to motivate salespeople to work harder and drive better results. Some strive to deliver on the desires of the different company stakeholders. For example:

- Salespeople want a plan that's fair and enables them to make money.
- Sales leaders want a plan that drives high levels of achievement.
- Human resource leaders want a plan that attracts, motivates, and retains the best sales talent.
- Marketing leaders want a plan that focuses sales activity on the right products and markets at the right price.
- Finance leaders want a plan that's fiscally responsible.

The reality is that there are many drivers of sales force success besides the sales incentive plan. People are not coin-operated; it's not as simple as putting a quarter in the vending machine and getting something out. Realizing better results from the sales force can require restructuring the sales team, hiring better talent, providing more effective coaching, creating a more motivating sales culture, and/or implementing changes to many other sales force programs. But these changes can take a long time to implement and can be very disruptive to the sales force. Companies gravitate toward the incentive plan because they perceive it as a quick fix; it strikes companies as an easier solution than some of the aforementioned programs. And it will get the sales force's attention.

Changing the incentive plan isn't always easy. Companies make a lot of mistakes with their incentive plans. They make it too complicated to understand, limiting its motivational value. They over-incentivize or under-incentivize key products, resulting in misdirected sales force effort. They underpay their top performers. They overpay salespeople who have territories with a lot of opportunity, and they underpay those in less favorable markets, thus paying for the territory and not the talent. They create plans that have unintended consequences—for example, plans that cause salespeople to engage in behaviors that maximize their short-term income while compromising customer focus and company success.

Companies also make mistakes when setting goals or quotas. They set quotas that are too low, so that salespeople far exceed them and earn a big payday without having to work particularly hard. Even worse, the sales force may expect that a high-pay-for-easy-work situation will continue indefinitely, and the company risks losing its best people if it sets more challenging quotas. More often, companies set quotas that are too high, so that people give up and stop working, putting off sales to the next pay period when they assume the quota will be lower.

Another classic mistake is making an incentive plan overly complex. I've seen plans that have payments linked to as many as 28 different objectives, as multiple market managers seek to gain sales force attention for their brands. One sales force selling to retail outlets launched a new SPIFF (Special Performance Incentives for Field Force) every week. People can't focus on that many things—three or four objectives is the maximum. A plan that can't be summarized on one side of a cocktail napkin is too complex.

A good sales incentive plan can be a key driver of sales force success. It motivates salespeople to work hard to drive results, and it ensures fairness by giving all salespeople an equal opportunity to succeed regardless of their territory. It provides strategic direction and aligns salespeople's activities with company goals and strategies. It pays for performance by giving the most successful salespeople the best rewards and aligning overall sales force costs with company results. In short, with the right sales incentive plan, a company can achieve better financial results, drive higher levels of quality sales effort, and create a motivated sales force with manageable turnover of sales talent.

How the World of Sales Is Changing

Creating an effective sales compensation program has never been more challenging than it is today. Sales jobs are undergoing dramatic change. Social media, email, videoconferencing, and webinars are giving companies new ways to connect with customers and prospects. There are more telesales and inside sales jobs, as well as more roles on national or key account teams. In many industries, the traditional role of the face-to-face seller is evolving to that of an orchestrator—someone in charge of managing all the different ways that customers can interact with the companies they buy from. In some ways, this means that individual salespeople play a diminished role in generating revenue, and this challenges two concepts that are critical to sales compensation planning: causality and measurability.

Causality suggests that you should only be rewarded for an outcome if you can affect that outcome. Does an individual salesperson *cause* a customer to buy when there is a 10-person team pursuing a contract? And, does a salesperson really *cause* a customer to buy something if that customer has already more or less decided what to purchase by reading web sites, reaching out to colleagues on social media, and getting questions answered through an online chat on the company's web site?

The other concept that is challenged is measurability: the ability to accurately measure the sales and profit generated by a single salesperson. As an example, if a salesperson is part of a large team serving a national account, it's difficult to measure the sales and profit impact of that single individual. Everyone may get paid on the aggregate performance of the account because we can't isolate individual impact. For traditional incentives to really work, you need to have causality and measurability, and in a lot of sales jobs those are declining.

In addition to sales roles evolving, the labor force is changing. Millennials have entered the working world in vast numbers over the last decade. Raised by nurturing parents, this generation of young workers craves frequent reassurance and feedback, and places high importance on meaningful work. Millennials grew up in a world of cell phones, text messaging, and social networks, and as a result, they have great technological savvy and an expectation of constant electronic communication. Contrast the needs of Millennials with those of the two other generations who have large numbers in today's workforce. Baby Boomers want to ensure a comfortable retirement. Generation X, in the middle, is working for financial security. Incentive compensation plans must accommodate all of these objectives, and designing a plan that motivates everyone in a diverse sales force is no easy task.

How Capabilities Are Changing

Companies can benefit from the many new analytic approaches and technologies available today to enhance understanding of incentive compensation and its role in motivating sales forces in the new and evolving world of sales. Advanced predictive analytics are helping companies get smarter about designing and supporting their sales incentive plans to drive results. These models go beyond traditional backward-facing analyses (Did last year's plan motivate the desired sales force behavior? Did we make our numbers last quarter?) and enable much more accurate projections about likely incentive plan performance in an unknown future. A few software and consulting firms are leveraging cloud-based analytics to examine data on incentive plan performance across many companies and to gain new insights about the impact of incentive plan design decisions on sales results. At the same time, software for supporting incentive plans is becoming more sophisticated. Mobile solutions distribute real-time performance information and scorecards across the sales force and engage salespeople and managers in driving sales results. More powerful and flexible administrative systems allow better tracking, diagnosis, and reporting on incentive plan performance, allowing companies to react quickly to changes in data or markets and to make timely course corrections.

As analytics and technology enable new possibilities for improving the impact of sales incentive compensation plans, researchers are studying issues that have high salience to incentive practitioners. New research focuses on a range of practical sales incentive plan issues—for example, how to design plan payout curves to boost the performance of core sales force performers (the middle 60 percent) and how to best motivate different generations of salespeople. At the same time, there is renewed focus on a classic debate: what should be the role of extrinsic motivators (such as monetary incentives) versus intrinsic motivators (such as meaningful and challenging work)? Some of this research suggests that the greater the complexity of the task, the greater the importance of intrinsic motivators. Despite the fact that many sales forces have built their culture around extrinsic incentives in the past, the implications of this research cannot be overlooked as sales jobs become increasingly complex in today's technology-enabled world.

Implications for Sales Incentive Compensation

Today's changing sales world calls into question the status quo in incentive compensation. Even though most companies will change their sales incentive plan this year, most of these changes will be evolutionary, not revolutionary. I hear many sales executives, compensation professionals, and sales operations leaders talking about the possibility of revolutionary change. But as of yet, I don't know of many companies that are doing it. Companies aren't sure what the future holds, and they continue to employ the same basic compensation strategies they have used over the last decade. Additionally, no one wants to be the first to implement radical change. For example, there's some argument that as a result of declining causality and measurability and the increased complexity of sales jobs, some companies are in a position where they should be moving a portion of incentive pay into base salary. But so far, companies largely haven't done that. They fear if they take away incentives, they'll lose their best salespeople.

When it comes to motivating salespeople, the time has come for a quicker pace for change. More and more companies are realizing this and crave innovation, yet most don't know what changes they could—or should—make. In *The Future of Sales Compensation*, Chad Albrecht and Steve Marley share insightful perspective about what lies ahead. As leaders in the sales compensation practice at ZS, the authors have a combined 25-plus years of experience helping companies design, implement, and administer motivational sales incentive compensation plans. Together, they have consulted with more than 250 companies in a range of industries across the globe, and their work has affected more than 150,000 salespeople. The insights they share from this broad perspective can help you become a sales compensation innovator and a leader in motivating your sales force to succeed in the exciting future world of sales.

Andris A. Zoltners
Founding Director, ZS

INTRODUCTION

~

If you do not think about your future, you cannot have one.

—John Galsworthy,
Swan Song

~

Brian Sinclair, senior director of compensation at US Foods, recalls a recent Google search he performed for "trends in sales compensation." "About five items down on the search [results] page, there's an incentives trends report from 2014," Sinclair says. "So I thought, 'Perfect—let's open it up and see what it is.' Do you know what it was? It was from a company in California, and half the slides were ones I wrote 10 years earlier when I was consulting to that company! Almost funnier was how, in the appendix, there was a reference to 'Tools for making good decisions about plan design that can help you in your *2011* planning.' But the cover of the report said 2014. I think their 'trends' were a little outdated! But it's no different at sales comp conferences. You go to sessions and often see old recycled slides with new titles slapped on."

Sinclair's story humorously illustrates a real concern: the lack of innovation in sales comp. And what he concluded from his Google search isn't so different from our experience; it is the reason we decided to write this book.

Our Journey

As sales compensation consultants, we've worked on projects with hundreds of clients over the past 15-plus years. Our focus in a very specific area for an extended period of time has given us lots of exposure to many different compensation plans at many different companies. We also travel frequently to conferences, trade shows, and association meetings to speak on, and hear about, sales compensation. These combined experiences have given us insights into patterns over time. In particular, we observed two things. First, little has changed in the area of sales compensation thought leadership. And second, while sales comp professionals often seem genuinely interested in new ideas, very few organizations are willing to implement radical changes.

Consider the following example: In 2014, we (ZS) were working with a company's Sales Operations and HR teams to redesign the sales force's incentive plans. As is the norm in these types of projects, we had formed a core team responsible for reviewing and approving plan design options, and the vice president of sales was part of that core team. He told the ZS team, "I'm looking to you to bring us ideas that maybe we haven't thought of. We want some out-of-the-box thinking." So that is what we did. After understanding the existing compensation plans, the data available, the sales force culture, the sales strategy, and the product drivers, we developed several different plan options, ranging from "evolutionary" to "revolutionary." As the names imply, the evolutionary plans tweaked existing measures and metrics to provide something that was safe (not a radical change) and easy to digest, whereas the revolutionary plans blew up the constructs, assumed no sacred cows, and were designed to kick-start the sales organization. Despite the vice president's assertion that he wanted "out-of-the-box thinking," perhaps not surprisingly, he chose the evolutionary plan, which made minor tweaks to the previous plan construct. The revolutionary plan was deemed to be "too different" and too much change for the sales force.

And this was not an isolated incident. Quota plans and commission plans evolve to become . . . quota plans and commission plans, all while sales leaders and compensation professionals speak of change. Such observations led us to wonder: Were companies serious about innovation and radical change? Or was sales compensation nearing the pinnacle of its evolution, with a future consisting of minor tweaks and incremental gains?

The answers are yes and no, respectively. So, if companies are serious about change, why aren't we seeing a more substantial advancement in the world of sales compensation? It is possible that sales compensation practitioners aren't sure what the future might hold. As a result, the best place to start—the safest place to start—is the past. The old adage "the devil I know is better than the one I don't" may apply when contemplating sales compensation plan changes.

Of course, in many organizations, sales leaders (and sales compensation leaders) don't want to rock the boat unless a specific event requires a more substantial change. A common fear is that changes to the incentive plan will upset top performers and cause an exodus from the company. Some organizational leaders fear that the new plan will actually get worse sales results than the current plan. "Why take the risk?" they may be thinking.

But perhaps it's possible to make substantive changes to improve the compensation plan without upsetting top performers. In fact, we believe the future of sales compensation is not in the evolutionary plan changes that so many companies employ today but rather in more revolutionary changes that will help both the organization *and* the salespeople (though many companies may take a more evolutionary path to get there eventually).

New Ways to Think About Sales Compensation

Admittedly, when we first started consulting with clients, even we had a narrow definition of sales comp. We sought to design plans that aligned with strategic objectives, motivated the sales force, rewarded performance, were fair, and hit appropriate pay-for-performance benchmarks while still being financially responsible. All these things are still very important—and even critical.

But the more we worked in sales comp, the more stagnant this limited approach seemed. Salespeople are not all the same, yet they are often portrayed as having the same personality archetype: type A personalities driven by cash and rewards. Despite believing strongly in the power of sales incentives, we began to wonder if designing the most effective motivational programs required more than dangling a carrot of "more dollars."

Why We Wrote This Book

As a sales and marketing consulting firm, ZS has a way of working: "Anytime you take something off the shelf, you need to improve it before you put it back." In other words, don't just use an existing methodology or concept without improving it. Our culture encourages us to innovate and change and get better every day. Our founders believe in the manufacturing concept of kaizen, a practice of continuous improvement that drove Japanese carmakers to the highest quality in the world in the late twentieth century.

Our Sales Compensation practice team lives the same values. As a result, we will not present any idea at a conference that is not new. New slides, new concepts, new project experiences, new ideas. We're trying to avoid the pattern that Brian Sinclair mentioned earlier of recycling old slides into a "new" presentation. While using old slides may serve sales compensation beginners well as they learn key concepts and practices, sales compensation professionals who want to know "what's next" are often left feeling unsatisfied. It's unsatisfying to us as well.

Take, for example, the concept of analytics. Some great analytics are done in sales compensation today, but almost all of them are "backward looking." We could have taken the backward-looking approach at the 2015 WorldatWork Spotlight on Sales Compensation conference and given attendees the payout statistics they should be striving for, along with some basic pay-for-performance analyses. But we chose instead to challenge that idea, look forward, and define a new way of thinking about analytics. We created and delivered a presentation on predictive analytics—the practice of looking forward and predicting future outcomes so that you can act on them. The result was a standing-room-only session at the conference—a tribute to the fact that sales compensation leaders in organizations are, in fact, seeking new ideas.

But innovation and prognosticating the future aren't just about coming up with new ideas. They also involve sorting through troublesome existing ideas that are causing turmoil in the sales compensation field. Take, for example, Dan Pink's book *Drive*, which we cover extensively in Chapter 1. When it came out in 2009, sales compensation professionals became very concerned about what it meant for their profession and, frankly, for their jobs. The book posited that extrinsic incentives were counterproductive for jobs that require cognitive thinking (including sales), and that companies would be better served moving solely to intrinsic incentives. If that actually happened, the entire sales compensation profession would cease to exist. Sales compensation professionals were all abuzz at conferences: the concept of moving away from extrinsic incentives didn't seem consistent with their experiences with the sales force. But they had no information or studies to disprove Pink's theory. We found comprehensive research that we were able to adapt and apply to sales compensation that provided a definitive answer on the topic.

This desire for change isn't one-sided—that is, it isn't consultants imploring organizations to be more innovative for our own benefit. We know sales comp leaders are looking for new ways to make their comp plans more engaging. They are hungry for ideas. We also know these same leaders are feeling pressure to be innovative and progressive given how diverse the workforce is becoming. For example, Millennials may be motivated in different ways than their more experienced co-workers.

We hope that readers of this book will get a vision for what sales comp could look like in 5 to 10 years and will be able to use that foresight *now* to develop new ideas, motivate their sales forces, create engaging sales comp programs, and drive better results. It's time to say good-bye to doing things the same way and to welcome a new era of sales comp innovation.

Who Should Read This Book

This book is written for anyone responsible for the design, communication, implementation, and administration of sales incentive plans, including sales comp directors, managers, and analysts. It will give sales comp practitioners forward-thinking ideas that will help them create better comp plans and drive superior performance within their sales forces.

This book will also be useful to sales managers and sales leadership. Sales compensation design teams often include several members of the sales organization. Being able to offer ideas or react to others' ideas with the research and thought leadership contained in this book will serve to improve the plan. And of course many in sales—as the ultimate recipients of such plans—like to read sales compensation literature to make themselves smarter about best practices (and usually to understand why their plan is not working!).

Bottom line: as with any professional vocation, it is critical to stay on top of the latest trends and to know where the profession is going. This book will help sales comp professionals do just that. Comp leaders don't want to be left behind, stuck in a sales comp rut, following the status quo, delivering compensation for a discouraged sales force. They want to be on top of relevant trends and research so they can stay ahead of their competition. And they need to know about the future of sales compensation so they can prepare for, and incorporate, the best ideas out there.

How the Book Is Organized

When deciding what we should cover in this book, we selected topics from multiple sources: client input, project experiences, academic studies, ZS research, and input from sales compensation professionals at multiple conferences. We selected the six topics that we believe have the most potential to materialize in the sales compensation field over the next 5 to 10 years. In some cases, these ideas have already begun to appear.

In Chapter 1, we tackle the fundamental question of whether salespeople need extrinsic incentives (for example, cash payments through a sales incentive plan). This has been a hot topic ever since Daniel Pink's *Drive* unveiled a new motivational model that is based solely on intrinsic motivation and eliminates extrinsic incentives. This idea caused sales comp to come under fire and briefly sparked a conversation within companies about disbanding their sales incentive programs. Most sales comp professionals knew instinctively that sales comp was unlikely to go away, but they struggled to argue against a popular book that suggested otherwise. In this chapter, we show research that supports both sides of the intrinsic-versus-extrinsic debate, and we describe how the most successful incentive programs in the future will balance both incentive types.

In Chapter 2, we compile and analyze some of the latest research that best-in-class companies should consider applying to their own sales organizations. Often we hear, "This is what worked when I was in sales" or "This is what worked when our company was growing rapidly," but these ideas were virtually never based on research and data about what has been *proven* to work. Part of the reason is that, until recently, there was not much data available, and much of it was academic and theoretical, making it difficult for sales comp managers to apply the data to their own situations.

In Chapter 3, we talk about how sales compensation plans are moving away from a "one-size-fits-all" approach to one that focuses on driving motivation through increasing levels of personalization. We explore the reasons for this shift, which include different generations in the workplace (Millennials and Gen Xers, for example), technological preferences and advances that support personalization, and an increasing amount of research to understand what truly motivates people. These factors are causing companies to rethink the traditional approach to sales compensation design.

Chapter 4 focuses on technology changes that are just now beginning to affect sales compensation. Today's rate of technological advancement is unprecedented, and software and technology will play a significant role in allowing compensation practitioners to make more strategic and timely decisions. Software applications designed to motivate the sales force will enable functionality that today seems far-fetched.

Chapter 5 discusses a relatively recent phenomenon affecting almost every aspect of our daily lives: predictive analytics. Netflix, Amazon, Match.com, and many other web sites use sophisticated analytics to predict and suggest choices. In the news, it has been reported that Amazon's "suggestion engine" is estimated to account for roughly 30 percent of the company's revenue. Yet a predictive approach is not generally applied to sales compensation analytics. The analytics we often see in sales compensation are tied to the past—backward-looking analytics that are not as helpful as they could be if they were more forward-looking. In this chapter, we examine how predictive analytics can be used by sales compensation practitioners to proactively add value to sales comp plan design.

Finally, in Chapter 6, we examine the topic of change management. We decided to discuss change management based on experiences with clients who tell us—constantly—that "sales reps don't understand the comp plan or how they're paid. Sometimes sales reps don't understand even what we would consider relatively simple plan designs." Why? Because companies spend less than 20 percent of their time rolling out the plan (compared to more than 80 percent designing it). More time should be spent on change management, which will help a new plan truly motivate behavior.

Our Goal for This Book

Our goal for this book is to provoke thought (and, we hope, engage readers with some real and relevant stories). We want to help sales compensation professionals think differently about how they design, implement, communicate, and support their sales compensation plans by painting a picture of what the future could look like.

We also hope to advance the state of the profession by changing the way sales compensation professionals do their jobs and how well they serve their companies' leadership. We wrote this book to unveil new frameworks, new stories, and new ways to think about sales comp. The book was aided in part from exclusive interviews with sales and sales compensation leaders from US Foods, CareerBuilder, Google, Xactly, Microsoft, Anaplan, and several other well-known companies who spoke with us about the state of comp affairs at their organizations.

We realize that not all of our predictions will be widely accepted five years out. Our aim is rather to inspire comp professionals to think about the future in new ways.

CHAPTER 1

Intrinsic versus Extrinsic Incentives: What Really Works?

~

Money was never a big motivation for me, except as a way to keep score. The real excitement is playing the game.

—Donald Trump,
The Art of the Deal

~

Rochester, New York, was once an epicenter of business. Not only was it the hometown of photographic film pioneer Eastman Kodak, but Rochester was also where the leader in xerographic imaging, Xerox Corporation, got its start. But for people working in sales, what really made this upstate New York town legendary was the 1970s sales force rivalry between Kodak and Xerox.

As the story goes, in 1976, Kodak had a staggering 90 percent market share of photographic film sales in the United States. The company employed thousands of salespeople and paid them a substantial base salary. Kodak's philosophy on sales compensation was to limit the amount of money salespeople could earn through incentives and instead focus on base salary and other job perks, such as a strong company culture and working for an industry pioneer and leader. Salespeople at Kodak had limited upside opportunity in their incentive plan, which capped the amount of incentive pay they could earn.

Across town, the Xerox name was quickly becoming synonymous with photocopying. Like Kodak, Xerox fielded an impressive workforce, but its philosophy on sales incentives was quite different and much more aggressive than Kodak's. Though Xerox offered a lower salary, top salespeople enjoyed higher incentive pay with no caps. Xerox's focus was to attract, retain, and motivate the best salespeople, and to do that, top-performing reps could earn well into the six-figure range.

News travels fast in small cities. It didn't take long for sales leaders at Xerox to learn who the best performers at Kodak were. The

Xerox managers would call Kodak's leading salespeople (those who had significantly exceeded quota that year) and ask them how much they earned in incentives. In a calculated attempt to lure Kodak's top performers, Xerox managers would reveal how much the salespeople *could* have earned with the same performance at Xerox. As a result, many of the best-performing salespeople left Kodak and joined Xerox.

Will Money Continue to Be King in 2020?

Intrinsic motivation involves completing tasks simply for the satisfaction the task provides. This could involve activities that provide a sense of achievement or an opportunity to learn and grow in a career, such as taking executive-level business classes. It could also include having more control over how salespeople spend their day, such as flexible work hours, or perks like General Electric's unlimited paid time-off policy for senior management that includes vacation, personal, and sick days.

The Kodak–Xerox example shows the degree to which extrinsic incentives ruled in the heyday of American salesmanship, allowing companies to attract employees with external rewards, such as money. But will future sales forces also be motivated by cash, or will we see a shift in motivational behaviors? Will salespeople of tomorrow be inspired to perform an activity for a personally gratifying outcome, such as recognition on a leaderboard or the chance to become an expert in a particular area?

Thought leaders have various opinions about the importance of intrinsic incentives in the business world, and some have even suggested that the best motivational model includes no extrinsic incentives and relies purely on intrinsic motivation. One book in particular, Daniel Pink's *Drive*, has been widely credited with significantly raising the volume on the intrinsic-versus-extrinsic conversation. The book uses a few academic studies on human performance to introduce a new motivational model that is based solely on intrinsic motivation and eliminates extrinsic incentives for cognitive tasks. (When we say "cognitive tasks," we mean those that are more cerebral in nature than rudimentary work tasks.)

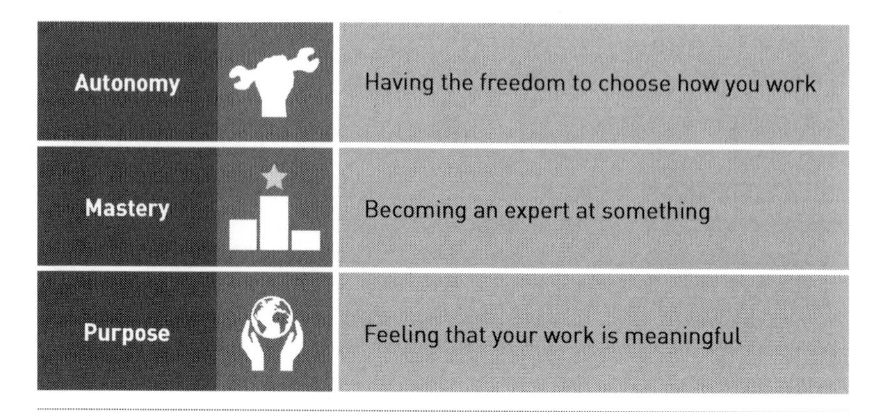

Figure 1-1. *Examples of intrinsic incentives*

The basic premise is that extrinsic incentives do not help in the completion of complicated, cognitive tasks—in fact, they hurt performance. Daniel Pink advocates for intrinsic incentives only, such as autonomy, mastery, and purpose (see Figure 1-1). So, are intrinsic-only motivational programs the wave of the future?

What Motivates Salespeople?

Before we discuss the use of intrinsic incentives in sales, let's start with one of the basic theories of motivation. In 1943, Abraham Maslow introduced his now-famous "hierarchy of needs." In his paper "A Theory of Human Motivation," published in *Psychological Review*, Maslow illustrates five unique human needs in pyramid form (see Figure 1-2). When one need is met, individuals strive to achieve the next higher need in the hierarchy.

In the early period of human existence, people were mostly in the lowest level of the hierarchy—they would perform tasks to satisfy basic physiological needs, such as eating, drinking, and sleeping. Their priority was to fulfill these needs.

Capitalism and the industrialized era moved humans up the hierarchy. As people evolved and commerce emerged, humans advanced beyond basic physiological needs to the next levels of "safety" and "love/belonging." Sales incentives in business were introduced to spur productivity, reward innovation, motivate selling behavior, and drive results.

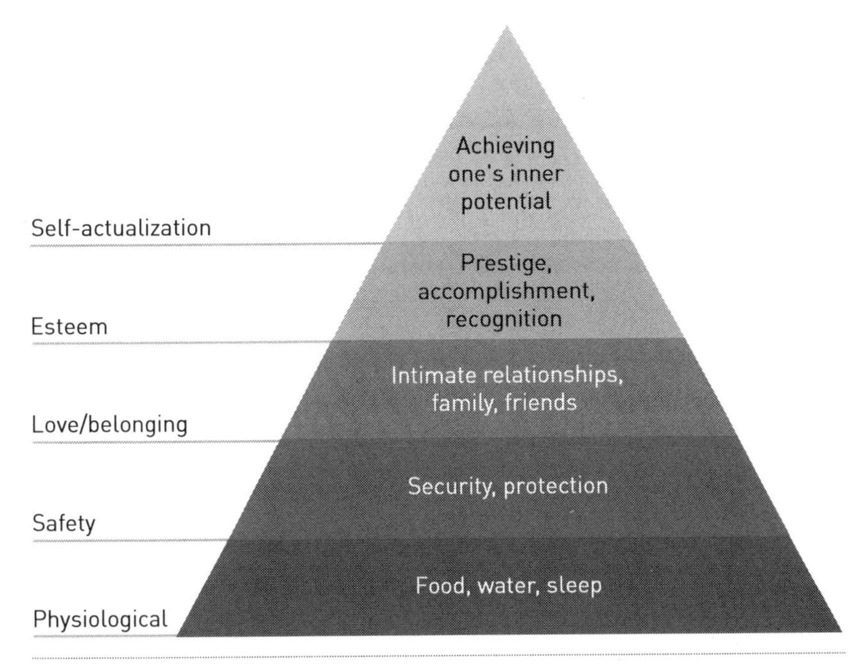

Figure 1-2. *Maslow's hierarchy of needs*

Are we now in a new era? Are individuals today collectively in the top two tiers of Maslow's hierarchy, motivated by intrinsic rewards, such as performing an action for the personal satisfaction of completing the task? If so, what does this mean for salespeople who, on average, earn 40 percent of their total cash compensation in incentives? Will intrinsic rewards replace extrinsic incentives in the future?

This last question has been of exceptional interest at sales compensation conferences following the publication of Pink's book in 2009. Sales compensation professionals wanted to know whether traditional ways of incentivizing salespeople would be phased out. Attendance at sessions dedicated to the topic of extrinsic versus intrinsic incentives was standing room only.

Most sales compensation professionals at these conferences believed that the thought of discarding sales incentives would be anathema to their company's sales force. The salespeople they worked with tended to be money-motivated, aggressive, risk-loving individuals who wanted a sales compensation plan where the sky was the limit in terms of cash earning potential. At least, the top salespeople wanted that. Many sales compensation professionals shared urban legends about years when salespeople were the highest-paid employees in their company—even earning more than the CEO—and how those urban legends continued to motivate the entire sales force.

But the concepts of intrinsic incentives (autonomy, mastery, and purpose) also rang true with these sales compensation professionals. Giving people autonomy over what they do, when they do it, and how they do it resonated with attendees. And this wasn't surprising. As Pink theorized, people are wired to be self-directed and autonomous, and companies that have a more autonomous working model are outperforming those that don't.

People also have an innate desire to continue to learn and to master certain specialties. Given that today's employees expect to stay in a job just over four years (according to the U.S. Bureau of Labor Statistics), employees want to make sure that they are well prepared for their next job by developing mastery in key skills. This is true at Google, which has a broad people-focused strategy, and sales comp strategy is merely one part.

"A Googler's motivation from money typically decreases over time, being replaced by other attributes such as career path, making an impact, and satisfaction with the content of their role," says Marc Schoenen, compensation director at Google.

Sales compensation professionals at the conferences did not believe that intrinsic rewards would completely replace sales compensation. Why didn't the model of intrinsic-only incentives feel quite right?

- Was it because the intrinsic-only concept in Pink's book didn't apply to salespeople?
- Was it because the studies mentioned in the book were not structured in a way that made them relevant to a sales environment?
- Or were the participants at these conferences simply stuck in an old way of thinking?

It was with this in mind that we sought to answer a key question: *Are extrinsic incentives as important to salespeople as they have been in the past, and will they continue to be important to salespeople in the future?*

Examining the Research

There are people who favor the theories of intrinsic rewards, and there are those who favor theories of extrinsic rewards. In looking at the research, both sides of the intrinsic-versus-extrinsic argument can produce studies that support their case. In fact, literally hundreds of studies have been done on motivation. Rather than spending time reading each study, we instead examined what the aggregate data show across all studies. We did this by reviewing meta-analyses—essentially "studies of studies"—that look at all the research and arrive at a conclusion about what all the data say.

When we reviewed the meta-analyses, we were interested in understanding whether extrinsic incentives are more or less effective than intrinsic incentives, and we wanted to understand how they interact.

One meta-analysis compared the level of motivation in the presence of intrinsic incentives, extrinsic incentives, or both. The analysis showed that intrinsic and extrinsic incentives *were actually additive*. In other words, the value of the extrinsic motivation combined with intrinsic motivation was higher than the value of either motivator alone. According to the author of the meta-analysis, Uco J. Wiersma, "The issue carries important practical implications because it suggests how financial rewards should be coupled with management policies which stimulate an employee's intrinsic motivation."

A second meta-analysis we reviewed showed that financial incentives clearly had a positive impact on the *quantity* of the work being done. And the analysis concluded that financial incentives had no negative impact on the *quality* of the work (meaning the existence of financial incentives did not cause the quality of the work to suffer).

Finally, in the most comprehensive meta-analysis we reviewed, researchers sought a definitive conclusion on what the research says about how the effect of extrinsic incentives differs between manual and cognitive work. The analysis confirmed that the existence of external rewards, such as financial incentives, had a positive effect on the ultimate outcome for cognitive tasks. Across all studies, the existence of financial incentives showed a 20 percent gain in the end result for cognitive work tasks.

The meta-analysis did show that one of Pink's assertions was correct—financial incentives had a higher impact on the manual tasks in the studies than on the cognitive tasks. In fact, the impact on the work outcome for manual tasks was 50 percent greater than for cognitive tasks.

But the cognitive work studies still showed a 20 percent performance improvement with extrinsic incentives, not the negative impact implied in the book. This means that the introduction of financial incentives does result in a tangible increase in performance, even for cognitive tasks.

Another interesting finding in this meta-analysis is that short-term incentives of less than a month had only a 20 percent impact across all studies, whereas long-term incentives of more than six months impacted performance by more than twice as much (44 percent). The majority of the incentives in studies cited in recent books and articles are short-term—measured mostly in minutes or hours. Sales incentives are almost universally long-term (mostly a full year).

Across all of these meta-analyses, we found three definitive conclusions:

- First, extrinsic and intrinsic incentives are additive and not an either-or proposition. Both should be utilized to maximize motivation of the sales force.
- Second, the use of extrinsic incentives has a positive impact on the quantity of work performed and does not sacrifice the quality of the work.

- Finally, the use of financial incentives has a positive impact on work outcomes even for cognitive tasks like sales, especially over the course of a 6- to 12-month sales incentive plan.

Looking Ahead

So, what do you do with all this information? First, don't abandon your sales incentives if you are challenged by a company leader who read a book citing a single piece of motivation literature. Many individual studies side with either extrinsic or intrinsic motivation. Instead, focus on the meta-analyses that we discussed in this chapter.

Second, ensure that your sales incentive plan is optimally structured, aligned with strategy, and easy to understand. This will guarantee that you are maximizing your incentive dollars to drive performance at all levels of the sales organization.

Third, focus on improving intrinsic motivations for your sales organization, but don't overcompensate for a lack of intrinsic motivation by doubling down on extrinsic incentives. The research clearly shows that these two types of incentives should be considered together; they are not an either-or proposition. For example, don't try to use extrinsic incentives to make up for a job role that lacks autonomy. Instead, look at how the job is structured and the way your sales managers treat your salespeople, and make adjustments if necessary. This is especially true as team selling continues to increase in prevalence and the resulting individual impact on the outcome blurs. The less impact an individual salesperson has on the ultimate sales results, the more important intrinsic incentives become.

Fourth, do not try to change the sales incentive plan when your salespeople believe that they can't grow and learn in the role and don't have the opportunity to advance their careers. Salespeople want to evolve and develop—in their product knowledge, sales ability, or management responsibility. Your sales incentive plan should supplement this motivation, not replace it.

Fifth, do not ignore the importance of good sales managers. If your sales incentive plan includes many metrics and attempts to reward virtually every single thing you want your salespeople to be doing, you likely have an issue with manager abdication. Some sales organizations have even developed a "vending machine culture" where to get anything from their salespeople they have to give them money. Your sales managers are a critical element in motivating the sales organization. Don't make up for bad managers with an all-encompassing sales comp plan.

And lastly and most importantly, be holistic when thinking about what motivates people. Focusing on just intrinsic rewards or just extrinsic motivations could cause staff turnover. For example, if you focus only on the extrinsic side of the equation, you may make your top performers happy in the short term, but why would they stay with your company if they can make the same money elsewhere and have a more satisfying work experience? Similarly, if you focus solely on the intrinsic side and salespeople can make more money at another company, you may be in the same situation as Kodak in the 1970s—and your best salespeople may leave to pursue better opportunities elsewhere.

To bring this into the twenty-first century, at the Chicago-based company CareerBuilder, the shift from monetary rewards to more intrinsic motivations occurred when the company made major changes to its go-to-market strategy, moving from an advertising volume approach to a more consultative customer-solutions approach. "In the advertising space I would say that our folks tended to be more 'coin operated' back around 2005," says Justin Ford, senior manager, sales compensation, at CareerBuilder. "I feel there is more intrinsic motivation now because our reps do like the challenge of solving clients' needs."

The CareerBuilder story bolsters this chapter's main takeaway: the future of sales motivation is an optimal combination of intrinsic and extrinsic incentives. It is not an either-or situation but a both-and proposition. Being excellent in both is the ideal way to maximize the sales force's motivation and the results they produce. The importance of intrinsic incentives is on the rise and should be addressed in every sales organization. However, focusing solely on intrinsic incentives at the expense of extrinsic incentives could be a pendulum swing that will cause you to lose top performers who can make more money elsewhere.

CHAPTER 2

Using Research to Better Motivate Your Sales Force

~

It is a capital mistake to theorize before one has data. Insensibly one begins to twist facts to suit theories, instead of theories to suit facts.

—Sherlock Holmes,
A Scandal in Bohemia

~

Executives at a multinational technology company—let's call it TechCorp—fondly remember the profitable days of yesteryear. Double-digit sales growth was the expectation, and salespeople regularly delivered it. The company continually expanded the variety and types of products it offered and barely missed a beat. TechCorp's sales executives told and retold stories of how they or their colleagues sometimes earned well into six figures (a very substantial amount at the time) thanks to a commission plan that paid a percentage of revenue for all products and services sold, with accelerators on revenue above quota. This incentive plan, TechCorp's leaders believed, was a huge part of their sales team's success. And it would be again—or so they thought.

Fast-forward to the present day. In an attempt to kick-start their sales, the company's leaders wanted to switch all reps to a commission plan similar to the one that made their sellers successful decades earlier. The multinational now had thousands of sellers, and implementing a commission plan similar to that of earlier times was surely the solution they needed. "Could you imagine the kind of motivation there will be in the sales force under a pure commission plan?" asked one executive.

But times had changed. Over the years, TechCorp had gone from mostly individual selling to selling in very large teams. Because of their clients' global reach and the company's huge array of products and services, some of its biggest clients had over 100 of the company's salespeople assigned to them. TechCorp's markets also had widely varying growth potential—for example, China was growing 40 percent annually, whereas the United States was in the low single digits. The growth of certain products was also varied. Some were aggressive-growth products, and others were mature—even declining—products. The thought of applying a commission plan across these widely diverse worlds was giving TechCorp's sales compensation leader a headache. He didn't think it could work, so he sought ZS's advice to support his case.

One of the first questions he asked us was what we thought of the executives' plan. Fortunately, there were lots of studies, benchmark data, and our own experiences as consultants to show that this was probably not a good idea. We could, in fact, definitively point to why the commission plan of years past would not work for most sales roles in TechCorp's current structure. We laid out exactly what would happen if they did implement such a plan, based on relevant research, theory, experience, and frameworks. The findings were then presented to the company's sales executives and business unit leaders. Any impact our guidance had on their idea was short-lived. TechCorp's leadership decided to implement the pure commission plan with a subset of the sales force to see if it would work. It was a failure, many of our predictions came true, and the plan was quickly abandoned.

This story illustrates the central theme of this chapter: the importance of using reliable, relevant research to challenge both the status quo and internal biases based on past experience. With so much research available today, it is no longer prudent to implement a plan just because the same plan worked 20 years ago. Rather, companies need to look to emerging data sources to see what kinds of incentives would work best for their sales forces and how the incentives should vary based on the sales role and the products being sold.

The purpose of using research and data is to ask if things that have been done in the past are the right things to do in the future. Sometimes the research validates a course of action, and sometimes it refutes it, as the example of the multinational tech company shows. Had the company's executives listened to what the research we found said about their idea, they could have avoided failure.

Metrics: Addition = Subtraction?

One area of research that we believe should be on your radar looks at whether it is smart to include every desired sales outcome in a plan, even if it means assigning a very low weight to some metrics. The book *Advances in Behavioral Economics*, which assembled the most important papers on behavioral economics published in the last several decades, discusses a study from Uri Gneezy and Aldo Rustichini. In the study, students were asked questions from a college admission test. For each correct answer, the first group received no money (we'll call them "cash-free"), the second group earned 2.5 cents (we'll call them "small-payout"), and the rest got a quarter.

The cash-free cohort scored 28 out of 50 questions correctly. The second, small-payout group managed only 23 accurate answers. And those receiving a quarter for each correct answer outperformed the others by quite a margin, with 35 correct answers (see Figure 2-1).

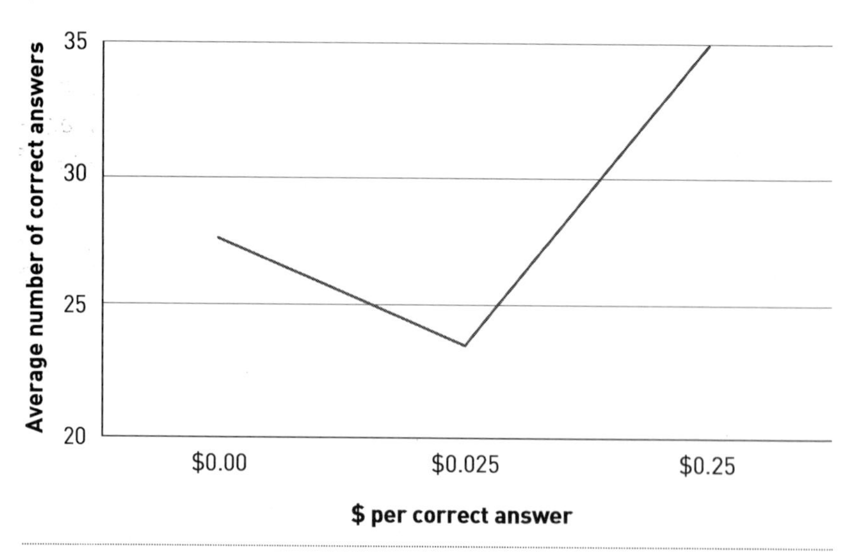

Figure 2-1. *Very small extrinsic incentive can replace intrinsic motivation*

Even without any extrinsic incentives, the cash-free group tried reasonably hard. Yet the 2.5-cents group earned the lowest score. Researchers believe that's because tiny, meaningless rewards can actually displace intrinsic motivation. In other words, humans expend effort because they feel inspired and/or because they're offered a great carrot or stick. But offering a very small carrot or stick may not be enough to motivate people, while at the same time eliminating or reducing the intrinsic motivation. In short, this is a lose-lose situation for companies: money is being paid for lesser sales performance.

Another key takeaway from this study is that you should not put everything in your sales incentive plan that you want your salespeople to do. In fact, you're less likely to get sales reps' attention on those components if they are a small percentage of the total. A base salary should warrant some behavior in return. And, equally, your sales managers should be coaching all elements of the job—even those with no incentives attached.

Components in your sales incentive plan should carry a minimum weight of 15 to 20 percent. Similar to the student example, incentive components with very small weights have little impact. Adding a component at a 5 percent weight may make a marketing manager for that product feel good, but the reality is that it will have little to no effect on the sales outcome.

And aim for no more than three metrics in your sales compensation plan. Xactly, which makes incentive compensation management software, analyzed sales performance for the hundreds of companies in their database (see Chapter 4, where we discuss Xactly's Insights platform in more detail) and found that once you go beyond three metrics, overall sales performance begins to decline dramatically. And the more metrics you add beyond three, the more sales performance continues to decrease. (See Figure 2-2.)

Based on an aggregation of relevant research and data, we believe that fewer metrics—and simpler plans—will dominate the future of sales compensation. Companies will need to focus their plans by limiting them to three metrics, all with meaningful weights. Rather than adding every desired sales outcome to a plan, companies will

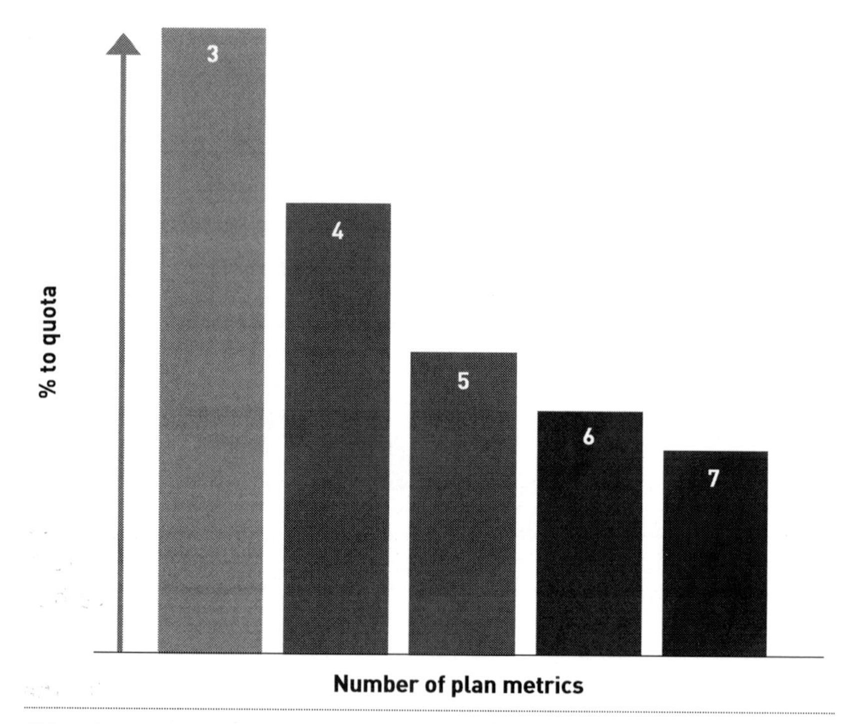

Figure 2-2. *Overall sales performance based on number of plan metrics*
Source: Xactly.

be much smarter about what is actually included and will place importance on getting additional sales outcomes via good managers and intrinsic motivations, such as recognition and flexible work hours.

The Importance of Fairness

The need for fair treatment is deep in humans' DNA. Research at Emory's Yerkes National Primate Research Center demonstrates this. One study involved the highly intelligent capuchin monkeys, which scientists value for their similarity to people. Psychologist Sarah Brosnan and primatologist Frans de Waal sat capuchin monkeys in cages where they could observe each other's behaviors. Experimenters then handed the monkeys rocks and gave a cucumber slice to those who returned the granite tokens. When all monkeys were offered this exchange, 95 percent completed the task. The rock-cucumber trade appealed to almost all the animals.

Next, in exchange for the token, some received more appealing rewards (grapes) in full view of those monkeys that continued to get a cucumber. Participation among those offered a cucumber suddenly dropped to 60 percent. The economic transaction hadn't changed for them—a token for a cucumber slice—but the sense of equity had. Over a third of previously cooperative monkeys opted out when they saw their "peers" receiving a tastier (and therefore greater) reward for the same effort.

In the final stage of the study, some monkeys were rewarded with grapes for doing nothing at all. Now only 20 percent of the token-for-a-cucumber-slice group was willing to exchange. The degree of unfairness had gone up (others were getting a greater reward for lesser effort), and with it, the willingness to participate had decreased for those treated unfairly. (See Figure 2-3.)

"What we're really testing is how do you respond when you're the one who gets the lower salary, not how do you respond when you

Effort	Reward	Unfairness	Participation
=	=		95%
=	↓		60%
↑	↓		20%

Figure 2-3. *The impact of perceived unfairness*

hear there's a discrepancy between salaries in the environment," Brosnan said during an interview with National Public Radio entitled "Monkey Business: Fairness Isn't Just a Human Trait." Brosnan continued, "[The monkeys] don't necessarily have to have an ideal of fairness or an idea of the way the world should work. All they have to care about is that they got less than someone else."

The same can be true for humans. If any inequality exists, salespeople sniff it out quickly. Sales reps talk among themselves, discussing base salaries and incentive pay (to the dismay of the Human Resources department). They know one another's quotas and sales opportunity, or at least they think they know. And they certainly hear about any special exceptions made for individual salespeople.

To avoid perceptions of unfairness—and the poor morale that results—savvy companies should do the following:

- Set individual quotas to reflect the relative opportunity for each territory.
- Ensure that all salespeople have a reasonable amount of "hunting ground" to make a living.
- Be more transparent than they are today about how quotas are set and why differences exist.

Additionally, forward-looking companies will become better at equalizing base salaries, especially in hot job markets where new hires often enter at pay levels higher than veteran workers. Companies historically have tried to minimize costs by not scaling up everyone's wages. Established employees are rightfully irritated to be outearned by newcomers without tenure—they see it as unfair. Much like in the capuchin monkey study, a transaction that was acceptable last week may not fly this week when the rewards differ among peers. This was seen when Wal-Mart raised its minimum wage across all stores but did not raise the wage of those employees who were already earning slightly above the new minimum. The predictable outcome: not adjusting everyone's wages resulted in reduced morale among the more tenured staff.

Unfortunately, this practice of not equalizing base salaries remains all too common. The complaint "To get a raise here I need to quit and come back" has been heard time and time again. To avoid low morale, disengagement, and turnover among experienced sales staff—especially strong sales performers—smart companies must look holistically at pay levels and not focus solely on rates for new hires.

Firms, and sales leaders in particular, will also need to be straightforward communicators. Authentic communication fosters relationships between employees and their supervisors and builds camaraderie. We are in an age where higher-ups who "spin" their corporate messages won't be trusted. It's the same distrust people have for politicians who carefully craft their messages based on what they think people want to hear.

"When I speak to field managers, I can't maintain my credibility if I'm not being transparent," said Steve Herz, who works in Global Sales Incentive Compensation Design at Microsoft. "You have to tell it like it is. The more spin, the more risk for loss of credibility."

A study by employee engagement consulting firm BlessingWhite reinforces the importance of real conversations. It found that managers who showed their "human side" rated higher on critical skills among employees. And in a research report published by the Society for Human Resource Management, one of the key criteria for job satisfaction was "overall company leadership." Salespeople want genuine and trustworthy leaders with integrity. If bosses spin facts to mask unfairness, salespeople will uncover the deception quickly, and it will be hard to regain their trust. But sales management's commitment to honesty and transparency is only part of the sales success puzzle.

The Benefit of Interim Milestones

Introducing intermediate deadlines and holding people accountable for meeting them has been found to be an effective motivator.

Duke University marketing professor Dan Ariely, author of *Predictably Irrational*, conducted an experiment across three sections of the same college course. He differentiated each group's deadlines to see how it affected the quality of the students' work.

For the first class, he allowed the students to set their own deadlines throughout the term for the semester's four assignments. He did not reward early submissions, but he imposed a grade-reduction penalty for late material. He told the second session that they could deliver all projects at the end of the term. They could submit early, if they wanted, with no reward or downside for doing so. For the third group, Professor Ariely set specific deadlines, as well as repercussions for missing them.

Afterward, the projects were graded by a teaching assistant with no knowledge of which category the students fell into, avoiding bias. Ariely discovered that the class with professor-imposed deadlines scored highest; the self-set deadline group came next, followed by the students who had no time constraints.

Those in the "choose your own deadlines" class seemed to recognize that they would be better off setting some interim deadlines, instead of leaving everything to the last minute. Not surprisingly, students without deadlines tended to wait until later to begin the assignments, were more pressed for time, and handed in poorer work.

Similar results appear in sales compensation research, especially for the bottom tier of performers. In a *Harvard Business Review* article co-written by University of Houston professor Mike Ahearne and University of Virginia professor Thomas Steenburgh, the authors discussed a study Steenburgh had done within a durable-office-goods sales force.

During the study, researchers introduced quarterly milestones (see Figure 2-4) into the plans for some populations, and others were simply paid on annual bonus plans. The researchers then looked at how the existence of quarterly milestones affected three different groups of salespeople: the stars (the top 20 percent of performers), the core performers (the middle 60 percent), and the laggards (the bottom 20 percent).

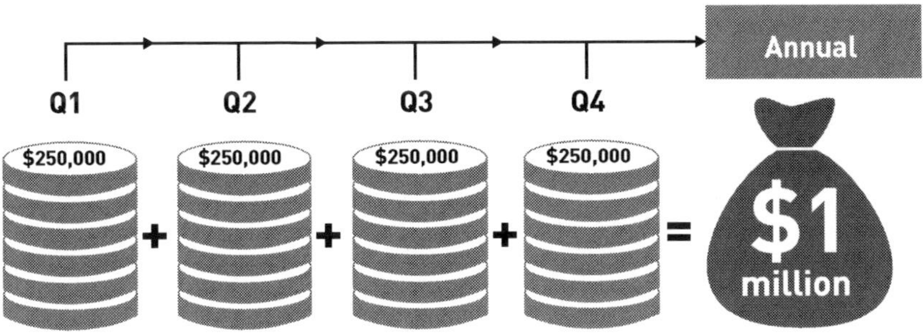

Q1 $250,000 + Q2 $250,000 + Q3 $250,000 + Q4 $250,000 = Annual $1 million

Figure 2-4. *Quarterly milestones leading to an annual goal*

Removing quarterly bonuses from the laggards' incentives—and keeping only an annual bonus—decreased their overall performance (as measured by revenue) by approximately 10 percent. In other words, having "interim milestones" would have increased the productivity of the lowest performers by approximately 10 percent.

Introducing a quarterly incentive for the other two groups also resulted in positive strides—though less so. The inclusion of a quarterly bonus had a positive 4 percent impact on the core performers and a positive 2 percent impact on the stars. Simply put, there is no downside to including quarterly bonuses: they help laggards contribute to the bottom line without detracting from the performance of other groups.

Both Ariely's academic research and Steenburgh's sales force study show the value of introducing intermediate goals and holding people responsible for meeting them. In doing so, companies can enforce self-discipline and maintain high levels of sales effort throughout the year. Going forward, wise companies will institute more milestones and will also measure, report, and pay on them regularly. As we saw in Steenburgh's quarterly milestones study, the aggregate effect of adding in the milestone bonuses was almost 5 percent across all three groups (cores, laggards, and stars), which would more than offset any additional sales comp administration costs. As companies look to get every dollar of output from their incentive spending, they cannot afford to ignore clear quantifiable benefits such as those supported by these studies.

Framing the Plan

As we've demonstrated, science can guide comp plan development. One of the more interesting research findings in the last several decades is how different individuals' reactions are to the exact same information posed in different ways. Take, for example, a 1981 experiment conducted by university professors Daniel Kahneman and Amos Tversky, which looked at the impact of positive and negative framing on decision making. Participants were told to imagine that the United States was preparing for a disease outbreak expected to kill 600 citizens. People were then broken into separate groups and given options for preventive programs. In the first group, they could choose one of two options:

- A: saving 200 citizens
- B: a one-third probability that all 600 would be saved, and a two-thirds probability that no one would be saved

Seventy-two percent of participants chose Option A and 28 percent picked Option B.

In the second group, researchers provided the same two options, but framed them in a completely opposite manner as compared to the first group:

- C: 400 citizens will die
- D: a one-third probability that no one will die, and a two-thirds probability that all 600 will die

In this framing, 78 percent of participants chose Option D and 22 percent chose Option C.

Based on the groups' responses, the researchers concluded that two equivalent comparisons can generate two very different levels of desirability based on how they are framed. To illustrate this, let's focus on Options A and C. Option A is equal to Option C—both offer an assurance that 200 people will be saved—yet significantly more people chose Option A over the alternative (Option B) as compared to Option C over its alternative (Option D). Why? Because Option C was negatively framed and Option A was positively framed. Participants' choices were swayed by how the options were phrased.

While we're not talking about something as serious as a fatal disease, it is clear that how the sales compensation plan is "framed" is critically important. When plans change, even a little, salespeople get nervous. Without data or reassurance to the contrary, salespeople often assume their pay is going down, or they assume they will have to work a lot harder to keep it the same. That's rarely the case, however. Most plan changes (90 percent or more in our experience) pay the same amount of money or more. But the way to earn those incentive levels changes as strategic objectives are reconsidered and what defines "high performers" is redefined.

Our client experience suggests that firms spend less than 20 percent of the time thinking about how to effectively "frame" and roll out the plan (communication, training, change management) versus more than 80 percent of time spent on other elements of plan design. The result is unsurprising—people don't understand the plan as well as they should and often adopt negative attitudes about it. We go more into the future of change management in Chapter 6 and how we think plan communication will evolve for the better.

In the years ahead, companies will invest more time in educating and training field sales teams regarding any changes. They will better frame how to earn incentives, the significant upside, and what determines a top performer. Follow-up reports will then support the rollout messaging and highlight successful salespeople in the plan.

More businesses will also provide a "what if" calculator so that salespeople can understand exactly what they need to do to earn specific incentive amounts. This tool can be part of an overall sales performance management platform, or it could be as simple as an Excel spreadsheet.

Going Deeper

In addition to the studies already discussed in this chapter, other research has provided much-needed proof points for the return on investment (ROI) of specific plan design features. Here are some examples:

- Additional research from University of Houston professor Mike Ahearne shows that going from two to three tiers (points on the performance curve at which payouts accelerate and there is an implied additional objective) significantly improves the sales of core performers (the middle 60 percent).
- Work by University of Virginia professor Thomas Steenburgh reveals that removing overachievement commission rates in an incentive plan drops revenue-performance among star performers by 17 percent.
- At the time of writing of this book, Ahearne is in the middle of research on how incentive effectiveness differs based on age and gender; the results could have significant impact on the way incentives are structured in the future.

Looking Ahead

Based on the studies done to date, we expect to see multiple comp plan changes:

- Elimination of meaningless metrics (weight less than 15–20 percent)
- Increased focus on quota setting and fairness
- More payout "tiers" immediately below and above 100 percent performance to drive the large group of performers "in the middle"
- Increased willingness to include accelerators in the plan
- Better plan communication "framing"

As more and better research continues to become available, best-in-class companies will monitor the latest findings and think about how to apply the research to their own sales organizations. This will ensure they don't miss out on research that could help them continually improve their sales incentives to maximize the incentives' effectiveness for their sales forces. Companies will also conduct their own internal studies of their sales organizations to learn which incentives work best. (In Chapter 3, we will go into more detail about the importance of doing internal research.) Sales compensation managers at leading companies can then analyze all of the data (external and internal) and put relevant findings into a coherent set of facts that will help drive the development of their comp plans in the future.

CHAPTER 3

Moving Away from One-Size-Fits-All Comp Plans

~

The person who follows the crowd will usually go no further than the crowd. The person who walks alone is likely to find himself in places no one has ever seen before.

—Albert Einstein

~

With a puzzled look on his face, Jay Graves, head of sales at a leading global diabetes medical device company, sat down after a long day of recruiting. Speaking with a number of MBA candidates who were interested in positions at the global healthcare leader, Graves began to recognize an interesting trend—one that eventually had him questioning the effectiveness of the company's sales compensation program.

In his conversations with the recruits, Graves found that he could identify two distinct groups of interviewees: those with previous work experience and those who went to business school immediately after undergrad. The latter group had very little, if any, job history and tended to be 3 to 10 years younger than the other candidates. The group with previous work experience spoke about the contributions they could make at the firm and the things they'd learned in their MBA programs, and *eventually* they spoke about their expectations for salary and incentives. But what struck Graves were the questions asked by the "no experience" group. They started their meetings by talking about their expectations for very high salaries, extended vacations, the ability to work remotely, and what the company would contribute to their careers.

Graves saw the writing on the wall.

"Change was coming," he said afterward. "You could choose to fight it, or you could find ways to adapt to it." Specifically, Graves realized that different types of workers wanted different things, which made him wonder: "Is money still the carrot that will really keep a sales force motivated and engaged?" Wisely, Graves decided to speak with the company's Human Resources department to understand what options were available to make working at the firm a more desirable experience for a wider range of salespeople.

Graves isn't alone in asking this question and wanting innovative ways to answer it. Many companies are thinking about how they will motivate their sales forces in the future, especially when dealing with a diverse workforce. Some companies have workers who want financial security. They may be close to retirement or may be new parents who need monetary stability for their families. Other companies employ a new generation of salespeople who place a high value on meaningful work, maybe more so than they want financial wealth. Then there are companies where the sales force is made up of stereotypical "salespeople"—the person for whom money is the prime motivator and sales compensation is king. More often than not, though, a sales organization is made up of many different personality archetypes—not just one! In such cases, we're left to question how traditional one-size-fits-all sales compensation plans (meaning a single plan construct applied unilaterally to an entire group) will survive in the future.

Changes to the Sales Compensation Environment

Sales compensation plans are typically designed with four objectives in mind:

- Attract and retain salespeople
- Motivate by generating excitement
- Direct behaviors
- Pay for performance

The desire to reward performance through monetary payouts, prizes, or recognition has probably been the most explicit and obvious objective of sales compensation. The ability to drive motivation in traditional sales compensation programs, however, was dependent on the belief that salespeople would expend more effort in the pursuit of higher goal attainments, commissions, and payouts.

Seeing the struggles Graves and other sales professionals are going through when managing compensation for a changing workforce, we believe one-size-fits-all plans will likely decline in relevance in the future. Differences in what appeals to dissimilar groups of employees are forcing companies like Graves's to diversify their comp programs. But generational changes, particularly with the increase in Millennials in the workforce—along with technological advances and improvements in motivational research—are causing companies to rethink the traditional approach of one sales comp plan per sales role.

The three trends of technology upgrades, generational changes, and motivational research advances are not new. In fact, a quick review of the past 50 years reveals the radical advances made in these areas. Figure 3-1 shows some highlights.

So, how will the continuing changes in technology and the workforce and advances in motivational research influence sales

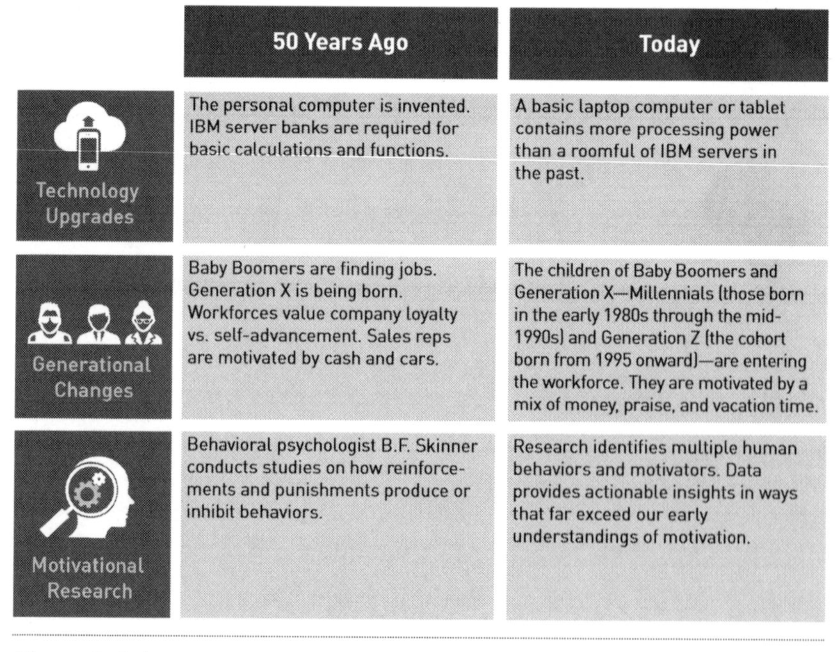

	50 Years Ago	Today
Technology Upgrades	The personal computer is invented. IBM server banks are required for basic calculations and functions.	A basic laptop computer or tablet contains more processing power than a roomful of IBM servers in the past.
Generational Changes	Baby Boomers are finding jobs. Generation X is being born. Workforces value company loyalty vs. self-advancement. Sales reps are motivated by cash and cars.	The children of Baby Boomers and Generation X—Millennials (those born in the early 1980s through the mid-1990s) and Generation Z (the cohort born from 1995 onward)—are entering the workforce. They are motivated by a mix of money, praise, and vacation time.
Motivational Research	Behavioral psychologist B.F. Skinner conducts studies on how reinforcements and punishments produce or inhibit behaviors.	Research identifies multiple human behaviors and motivators. Data provides actionable insights in ways that far exceed our early understandings of motivation.

Figure 3-1. *A comparison of trends impacting sales compensation*

compensation in the future? In the next sections, we explore these three trends in detail and discuss the reasons they are causing sales executives like Graves to reexamine their comp plan offerings.

Trending: #TechnologyAdvances

To illustrate how significant the impact of technology has been, and will be, on sales compensation, let's travel back to the 1950s and reminisce about sales compensation in its earliest form. Remember the days when there was a knock at the front door from a well-dressed salesperson wanting to sell your mom (or grandmother) practically anything your family could use, from a shiny new vacuum cleaner to a case of encyclopedias? In some respects, the early salesperson had a much easier job than the salesperson of today. The yesteryear sales rep was the main mechanism connecting consumer and product. He or she was the definitive source of detailed information about the product, and his or her ability to inform and educate the consumer and differentiate the product played a major role in the sale. In addition, because the early sales reps were working on commission, their rewards were tied to sales performance in a simple manner: sell product X, receive a commission of $Y. In the era of door-to-door sales, it was relatively easy to pay individual salespeople based on performance: the line of sight to, and responsibility for, the sale was clear.

But the sales process has changed dramatically. Present-day buyers rarely rely solely on salespeople for information vital to the purchasing process. In fact, a Corporate Executive Board study estimates that 57 percent of the purchasing decision is made before a buyer even speaks with a salesperson. So if the buyer isn't dependent on the sales rep for a product's pros and cons, where does the buyer's knowledge about the product come from? In most cases, consumers are collecting product or service information on the Internet. In the past, for example, the salesperson held all the cards when it came to data about a vacuum cleaner's effectiveness in removing dirt. But today, consumers can instantly google the product's reviews before making a purchasing decision. They can use web sites like Cars.com, Amazon, and Redfin to educate themselves on available goods. Or they might find sites like Consumer Reports, Angie's List, and Yelp to be helpful, which don't just provide services and products to consumers but also publish user-generated reviews.

When it comes to the seller-buyer dynamic, information asymmetry—a term coined by economist George Akerlof to refer to an imbalance in knowledge between two parties and the resulting flow of power in that relationship—has certainly shifted. The power now resides with the consumer, who can quickly search online for a product, find and read reviews, and be influenced whether to buy an item based on users' comments, all within minutes, if not seconds. Buyers no longer have to take a seller's word with respect to a product's benefits.

Ironically, the poor reputations of certain early salespeople providing misleading information—think of the stereotypical "used car salesman" trying to pressure a confused consumer into an unnecessary purchase, like undercoating or paint protection—manifest themselves today in the form of fake online reviews. Bing Liu, a University of Illinois computer scientist, studies inauthentic reviews and estimates that around 30 percent of online rants and raves are fraudulent. Even popular web sites, including well-known travel planning sites, are experiencing public trust problems as consumers are wising up to the artificial nature of unverifiable reviews from people they don't know.

Thankfully, some companies offer technology that's the equivalent of a modern-day honest salesperson. For example, Angie's List's value proposition and tagline—"Reviews you can trust"—resonate with consumers, in part because of our collective concerns regarding the veracity of online reviews. At Angie's List, the support staff validates the reviews (and the reviewers) with follow-ups and confirmations to ensure that the various service providers (contractors, dog walkers, automotive repair shops, etc.) are accurately and fairly rated. This benefits other members, who can trust the Angie's List online community. (Requiring a nominal, annual membership fee also helps Angie's List ensure the legitimacy of the reviewers.)

While the availability of online purchasing information imparts power to the buyer, it raises questions about the role of salespeople in today's information-savvy world. How can sales reps benefit from, or be disadvantaged by, these technology upgrades? And how can companies keep their sales forces motivated to sell in an environment where it takes a consumer only 0.02 seconds to bring up 10 million search results or product reviews on a smartphone? The amount of information transmitted over the Internet is staggering (see Figure 3-2). We are becoming more and more connected, and can find answers to questions more easily than ever before.

So is technology the Grim Reaper of the salesperson? Fortunately, no. The rise of technology will not replace the need for human salespeople, but it will change the types of sales roles that are required and the way consumers derive "value" from salespeople. Because consumers can find and purchase products and services online, we can expect a marked decline in the number of people in traditional, transactional sales roles ("traditional" being defined as those sales roles whose primary function is to communicate a product's features and benefits). We will see an increase in selling roles that either provide value to consumers above and beyond

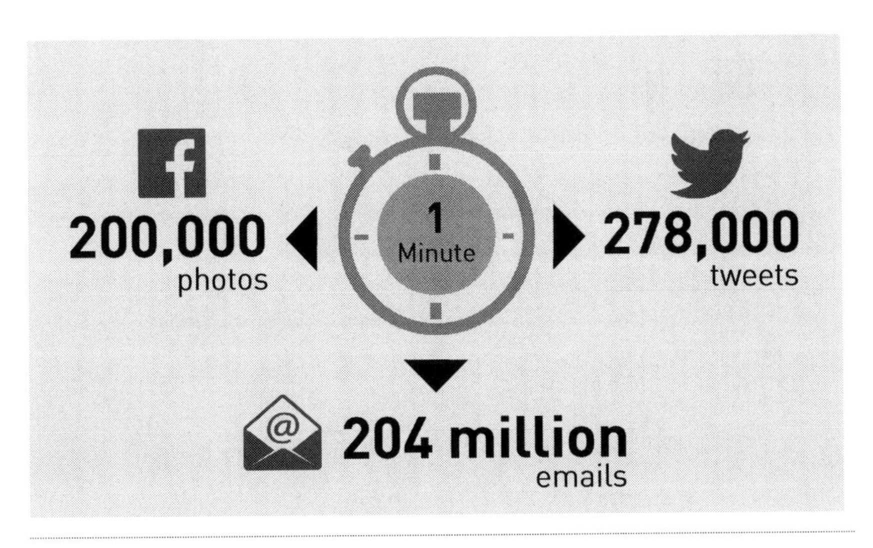

Figure 3-2. *Amount of information transmitted over the Internet in 1 minute alone*

purveying information or reach consumers in more economical ways. For example, we continue to see increases in the numbers of key account managers, strategic account managers, and inside sales teams.

But as much as technology is changing the face of sales, it is also empowering new and exciting advances in sales compensation operations and administration. We'll talk about technology's role as a sales enabler both later in this chapter and in more detail in Chapter 4.

In addition to advances in technology impacting sales roles, sales processes, and sales compensation, Millennials and the next generation of employees, Generation Z, are joining the workforce in increasing numbers, putting additional demands on employers and raising questions about the effectiveness of the time-honored tradition of incentives.

The Age of Entitlement

In 2010, Paul Harvey, a management professor at the University of New Hampshire, published a paper on the different expectations across generations. He found that members of Generation Y, now known commonly as "Millennials," scored 25 percent higher than respondents ages 40 to 60 and 50 percent higher than those over 61 years of age on measures of narcissism and psychological entitlement (see Figure 3-3 on the next page). As Harvey says, this "involves having an inflated view of oneself, and managers are finding that younger employees are often very resistant to anything that doesn't involve praise and rewards."

Additional research from San Diego State University professor Stacy Campbell and Kennesaw State University professor Jean Twenge, published in the *Journal of Management*, shows that Generation Y workers expect high salaries and generous amounts of leisure time. (Certainly, Jay Graves experienced this firsthand in his recruiting trip.) This seismic shift in expectations may have far-reaching implications, especially as the U.S. Census Bureau's labor statistics predict that 44 percent of the workforce will

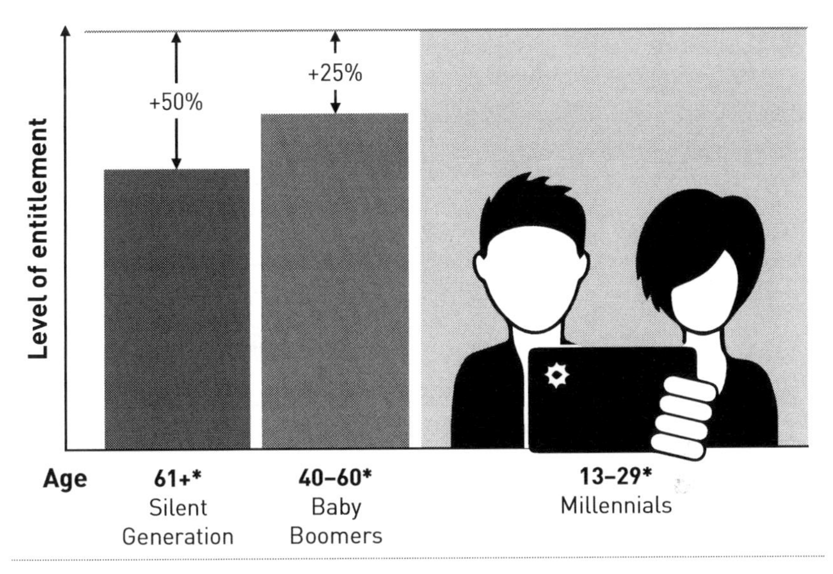

Figure 3-3. *Level of measured entitlement across generations*
*Ages in 2010.

consist of Millennials by 2020 (see Figure 3-4 on the next page). Sales comp leaders can only imagine how this new generation of employees will require changes to the way companies approach sales compensation. Traditionally, sales compensation operated with a "carrot and stick" model: succeed and be highly rewarded; fail and get little, if any, reward. Obviously, a generation not accustomed to faltering (or even being told that they underperformed) may not react well to this paradigm.

Does this suggest that sales compensation for Millennials only needs to provide upside, with no chance of earning less than target pay? Or will compensation plans always pay from dollar one? The answer to both questions is clearly no. Sales compensation practitioners will need, however, to develop new strategies that resonate with a different type of worker. In some cases, companies may choose to develop plan options that limit downside risk, or perhaps—as we discussed in Chapter 2—take advantage of tiering and milestones to keep people motivated and focused on that next incremental performance gap. Advancements in research about what spurs human behavior can also provide insights into how to design future sales compensation programs for a changing workforce.

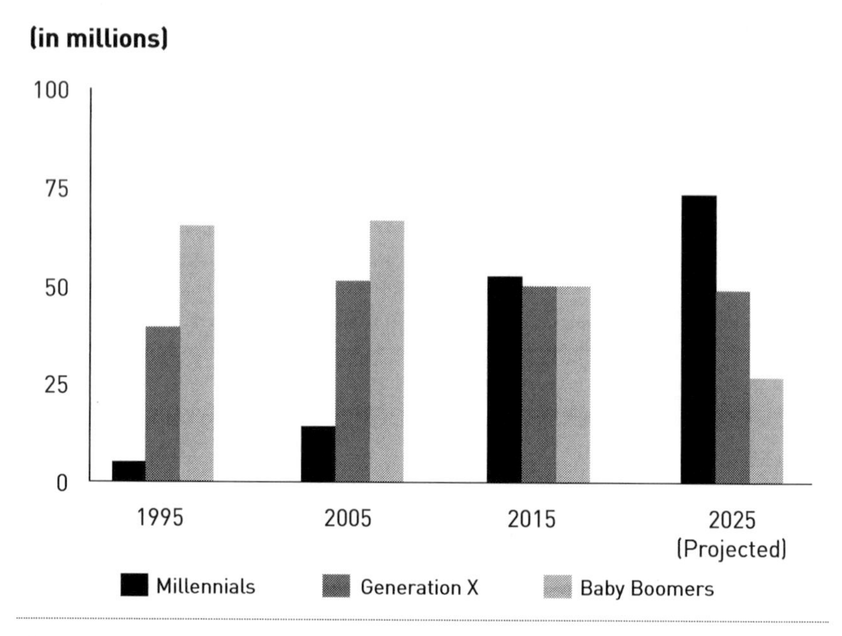

Figure 3-4. Workforce population trends by generation

What Motivates You?

Earlier in the chapter, we discussed four primary objectives of a sales compensation program. One of those is the expectation that the compensation plan will help motivate the sales force and generate excitement such that reps put forth maximum effort. But what exactly motivates the sales force? Before we answer that question, let's discuss how motivation works, in theory. Using a simple framework, Victor Vroom (a coincidental yet highly appropriate name for someone involved in motivational research), a professor at the Yale School of Management, suggested that motivation can be summarized in three basic steps:

In Component 1, a person decides how much effort to exert based on an expectation that his or her effort will translate into performance. In Component 2, the person must believe that the performance will turn into rewards (see Figure 3-5 on the next page). And in Component 3, the person needs to value the resulting outcomes.

We could spend entire chapters on Components 1 and 2 as they relate to sales compensation. In the interest of brevity: when it

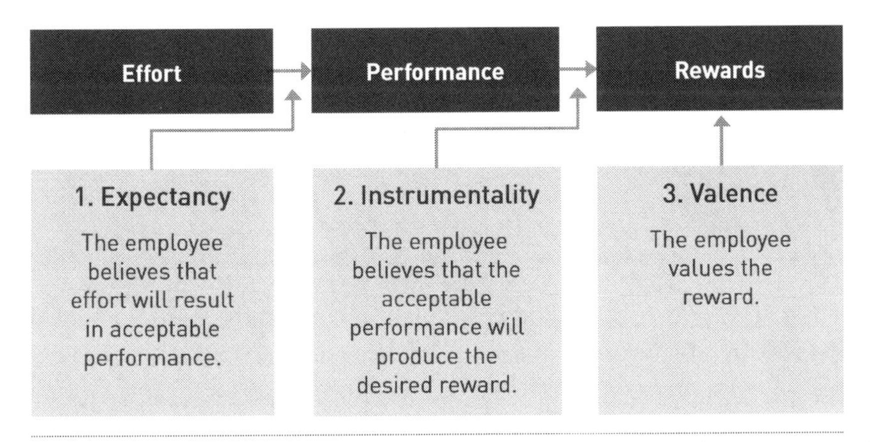

Figure 3-5. *Vroom's expectancy motivation theory*

comes to expectancy (Component 1), does the salesperson believe that his or her efforts will lead to sales, or are other external factors impacting the salesperson's ability to close deals? For example, in the pharmaceutical industry, companies may struggle to define the true impact of a sales call on a doctor, when payers and insurance companies influence which products are ultimately dispensed to the patients. Similarly, when it comes to instrumentality (Component 2), does the compensation program have variable pay elements that adequately reward performance? (To learn more about Components 1 and 2, we recommend reading ZS's *The Complete Guide to Sales Force Incentive Compensation*.)

We do want to spend time discussing Component 3—valence—ensuring that the outcome reward is valued by the salesperson. Not everyone values the same things equally, so companies should strive to have a clear understanding of what motivates their individual salespeople. (This is especially true given how diverse the workforce is becoming, with some workers motivated by money, and others motivated by a sense of purpose.) Maslow's hierarchy of needs (discussed in Chapter 1) is one of the most widely known theories of motivation. In it, he describes how human needs gradually progress from base physiological survival requirements to self-actualized wants. However, this theory lacks some of the specificity that would be beneficial in a business or sales context. As a result, many other researchers have put forth motivational theories that can be applied within the context of the twenty-first-century business environment. For example, author Daniel Pink's motivation model has gained considerable exposure in business and sales circles. It suggests that today's and tomorrow's employees want their jobs to provide autonomy, mastery, and purpose—core elements necessary to foster intrinsic motivation.

Another theory of motivation comes from the work of Paul Lawrence and Nitin Nohria, Harvard Business School professors who proposed that four fundamental drives dictate human behavior. These drives—to acquire, to bond, to defend, and to learn—speak to a variety of both intrinsic and extrinsic motivations. They are not exclusive and occur in differing degrees in different individuals: one person may be spurred on almost exclusively by a zeal for acquisition, while another may care about each drive equally. Lawrence and Nohria's framework is helpful in understanding future sales compensation opportunities because it acknowledges humans' complexity and more holistically describes the multifaceted drivers that shape human behaviors. Compensation programs of the future will offer "rewards" to salespeople based on a deeper understanding of the nature of human motivation.

Moving Toward Engaging, Motivating Plans

The sales compensation programs of today should be able to deliver results better than ever, thanks to a greater understanding of what motivates individuals, more insight into generational differences, and advances in technology. As compensation programs evolve, plans will need to do a better job of "speaking to the salespeople" and resonating with them. To do this, companies are beginning to acknowledge that workers are individuals and derive inspiration from many different incentives. In the past, companies often employed a one-size-fits-all comp plan that centered on money as the key motivator. Sales leaders who worked in an era when money was the primary motivator may believe that every salesperson is similarly incentivized. ("I am motivated by money; therefore, my salespeople will also be motivated by money.") But today's sales forces—and the sales forces of the future—aren't necessarily motivated by the same things as their more senior counterparts, and they aren't afraid to speak up and demand customization.

As a result of the increasing demands and expectations of sales comp, we expect to see growth in at least three key areas in the future:

- **Increasing use of gamification**, where companies make sales compensation programs more fun to appeal to a younger generation
- **Tailoring of incentive plans**, where companies designate reward plans for individuals and groups based on multiple factors to maximize motivation
- **Providing choice of plans**, where salespeople can select from several plan metrics, performance measures, or payout mechanisms based on personal risk-reward profiles

The Power of Games

Sales compensation and game play share two objectives: to motivate and to reward participants. Although both accomplish those objectives in different ways—one through financial incentives or recognition and the other through game play—gamification seeks to tie them together. As a result, interest in gamification—the use of game mechanics in non-game situations—within the field of sales compensation has increased substantially in recent years. But is gamification in sales compensation a fad or a longer-term trend?

In 2014, Gartner, a research and advisory firm, stated that gamification was in the "trough of disillusionment" in the Hype Cycle (Figure 3-6), a period of time when interest wanes as implementations fail to deliver on the initial promise and excitement. (Gartner created the Hype Cycle concept to represent the maturity, adoption, and social application of specific technologies.) During this time, producers of technology shake out or fail. This seems almost inevitable for gamification software. An online search in

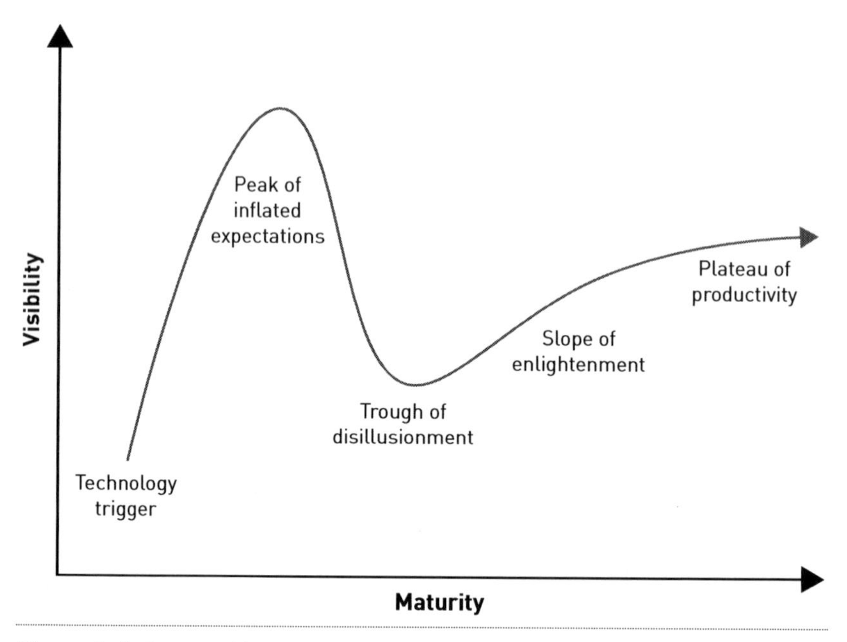

Figure 3-6. *Gartner Hype Cycle*

Source: Gartner Methodologies, www.gartner.com/technology/research/methodologies/hype-cycle.jsp.

2015 revealed over 40 companies with gamification software. Many of these software applications are basic or offer undifferentiated functionality. Some companies are hoping to catch the initial wave of excitement for gamification; others may be hoping to be bought. (For example, in 2015 Microsoft bought Incent Games, Inc., to include within its own Dynamics CRM platform.) One thing is certain: not all of the current gamification vendors will survive. Even so, we believe that the use of games is not going away even if some of the current providers fail.

Why will many gamification companies fail? The simple answer is that, as noted, many current game-play software applications are undifferentiated. Many of the present-day approaches center on themes—like golf, car races, basketball, etc.—presented simply as wrappers around leaderboards, with no real, lasting motivational value (see Figure 3-7 on the next page).

In the 1950s, statistician W. Edwards Deming found that quality improved simply by observing and reporting results. That has led

Figure 3-7. *Sample game leaderboard*

to companies creating and publishing leaderboards to improve sales performance. Many of today's gamification vendors use leaderboards and cite the competitive nature of sales reps and their desire to be at the top as a reason why game-play works to motivate salespeople. However, these types of "stack-rank and report" games have a shelf life, and the marginal, incremental energy and excitement wear off over time.

Consider behavioral change in the game-themed leaderboard of today. The desired outcome may be to increase revenue or to advance opportunities by one stage in the pipeline. In these situations, companies stack-rank the performance of the salespeople on these measures and display the results on the leaderboard, with the expectation that salespeople will do something differently to move up the rankings. (If no one does anything differently as a result of seeing the leaderboard, then the game has failed.)

Games in the future will be more than leaderboards and will be used to shape rep behaviors. For a template of what games will look like tomorrow, we turn to Jane McGonigal, author of the best seller *Reality Is Broken: Why Games Make Us Better and How They*

Can Change the World. McGonigal maintains that true game design goes beyond a list of victors and must contain four elements:

- Goals
- Rules
- Feedback
- Voluntary participation

Now think about behavioral change in the way that McGonigal envisions. She has used her four game-design elements to create a variety of games, from those that encourage young people to call their grandparents more often, to those that entice visitors to linger in cemeteries (an increase in visitors boosts funding and helps maintain the grounds). The purpose of McGonigal's games is to change behavior. It is this element of gamification (behavioral change) that will survive and thrive in the future with respect to sales compensation.

McGonigal's introduction of the concept of "voluntary participation" stands apart as something that would be unique in the world of sales compensation. Voluntary participation is a critical factor in game play (otherwise, the "game" may feel just like work), and it is a significant way to ensure behavioral change. For sales comp leaders, behavioral change is what will drive the main difference between the current approach to gamification software and tomorrow's true game design.

So what could future sales compensation game play look like? In an extreme situation, it could replace payouts—workers would sell because of the game, not because of some expected cash compensation. That seems unlikely given the general culture of monetary rewards and recognition present in most sales forces. Gamification (which involves intrinsic motivations) and extrinsic rewards can work side by side, as we discussed in Chapter 1. Instead of replacing monetary rewards and recognition, we believe gamification will be more heavily utilized to drive behaviors that in turn boost sales performance. Games will entice people to modify their selling activities because it's fun and part of a game—with the ancillary benefit to the company of increased sales.

Gone will be the days when "gamification" is a wrapper on results or when sales leaders try to change behavior by putting a measure in the compensation plan. (A day will come when sales comp designers will reminisce, "Remember when companies paid people to enter data in the new CRM system?") Games will be a powerful motivator that will, through virtue of voluntary play, get salespeople on the path to success, even if that success is still rewarded with cash payouts. Play will be the means, not the end.

In the meantime, games link to the three trends (technology upgrades, generational changes, and motivational research advances) we discussed in this chapter:

- Technological changes are enabling the rapid deployment of games, and software advances will soon give sales comp leaders the ability to create and customize game apps quickly.
- Millennials and members of Generation Z are more likely to play games than to read a book or watch a movie.
- When properly designed, games have the ability to change the way people are motivated by providing a series of small, incremental rewards that may not come from payouts at less frequent intervals (e.g., quarterly).

Creating Tailored Incentive Plans

Let's contemplate how sales compensation plans are created. The initial starting point for most plan designs is a job description and an understanding of the company's sales strategy. From those two pieces of information, the plan metrics and measures begin to take shape. For example, a company may decide to create an inside sales role, with salespeople responsible for lead generation. A compensation plan is developed that pays the telesales person a set commission for each lead that is passed on to and closed by the selling partner.

However, this approach often overlooks how motivating a plan actually is to the salespeople. Compensation has traditionally anchored itself around generalizations, like "Salespeople are motivated by money. Therefore, compensation plans that offer more cash will increase sales effort and reward results." While Chapter 1 showed that salespeople can be extrinsically motivated by cash and recognition, sales leaders like Graves are now looking to create plans tailored to individuals or groups, using a mix of reward mechanisms.

In 2014, ZS conducted a compensation study with the sales force of a large pharmaceutical and medical device company. The goal was to determine whether it would be necessary or beneficial to segment the sales team based on broad reward preferences. Using a modified version of the Four Drives Theory of motivation (to acquire, to bond, to defend, and to learn), ZS created a sales force assessment to determine whether salespeople were homogeneous in their reward preferences.

Traditionally, comp programs have almost exclusively focused on the drive to acquire, which includes both monetary rewards, such as cash and prizes like cars, and nonmonetary rewards, such as recognition programs. This drive was certainly prevalent with the first team that participated in our assessment. This team was focused on profitability, and its salespeople typically were older, had longer tenure, and were more experienced. This group expressed an 85 percent preference for monetary rewards (drive "to acquire") and only a 3 percent preference for bonding behaviors. But the second team was focused on customer service. Its members had shorter tenures and were generally drawn from the healthcare field. This group had an almost equal preference to "bond and belong" at 29 percent and to "acquire" at 33 percent (see Figure 3-8). Both groups had the same compensation plan, which wasn't well received by the team with the much stronger "bond and belong" preference. The outcome of this reward preference survey allowed us to shape recommendations to differentiate the company's compensation plans across the two teams.

A similar type of assessment can reveal the motivational preferences of your sales force, allowing you to design customized

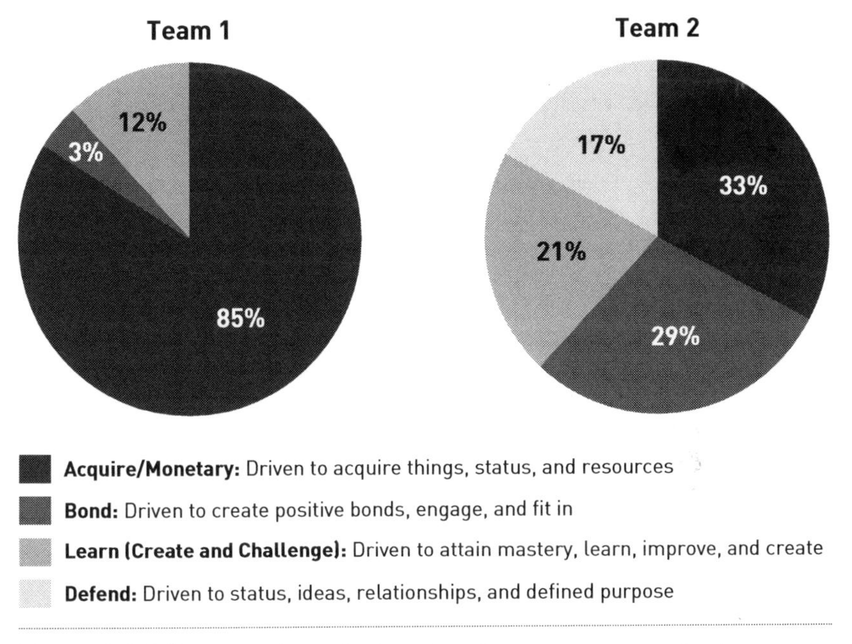

Figure 3-8. Differences in motivational preferences across sales teams

compensation plans that drive better results. Don't be deterred by the fact that the inclusion of personal preferences will initially create complexity when designing plans. New technologies will soon automate this process, reducing the burden on sales compensation designers and administrators. We will discuss some of these new tech tools in Chapter 4.

Pick Your Own Plan

In the previous section, we described a rewards preference survey we used to determine employees' preferences for our plan design recommendations. We recommend that Sales Comp, Sales Ops, Finance, and other departments consider preferences when designing plans and assigning them to roles, teams, subgroups, or even individuals.

A natural extension of considering preferences in plan design is a situation where salespeople have the ability to "Pick Your Own Plan" (PYOP). The PYOP approach supposes that maximum motivation will be derived when individuals work within a structure they have selected. Consider a simple example with three reps: John, Sally, and Tom. John is a 53-year-old salesman with almost three decades of experience. He has three kids, two of whom are in college. Sally is a 35-year-old with 12 years on the job. Married and child-free, she is considering taking evening business classes. Tom, a 24-year-old single man, shares a rental apartment with two friends and only began selling two years ago. John, Sally, and Tom do the same sales job and are all on the same goal-based plan, which pays based on a payout curve with a high threshold and reasonably high upside earnings opportunity. Will this homogeneous plan design have the same motivational impact on the three sales reps? Probably not.

Now, imagine instead that John can move to a goal-based plan that has less upside, but also fewer dangers—probably a good choice for a person needing a guaranteed income. Sally might keep her goal-based program but elect for a nonmonetary reward like time off or tuition reimbursement. Meanwhile, Tom could roll the dice on a high-risk, high-reward commission structure since he's young, he has no dependents, and shared housing keeps his costs low. Giving John, Sally, and Tom the opportunity to customize their own comp plans could motivate them to work harder and drive better results—or it could backfire.

Critics of the PYOP approach generally cite four concerns:

- **Buyer's remorse.** A salesperson picks a plan and then—after performing at a certain level—wishes he or she had chosen differently. Motivation falls because the individual sees what he or she could have had, from either an increased upside or a protected downside.
- **Potential inequity.** The difficulty lies in ensuring, in current sales compensation vernacular, that each sales rep has equal earning opportunities. Is Tom's commission plan equivalent to Sally's program in terms of upside? And how do her nonmonetary rewards compare with John's lower-risk profile?
- **Complexity.** It's challenging to model and administer multiple options, not to mention the need to tie expected performance back to a national sales number.

- **Maximizing motivation.** Will salespeople select a goal or plan that motivates them to stretch? It's possible salespeople will default to something they think they can easily accomplish rather than what the company would hope to get from them.

What does "buyer's remorse" look like? Consider the analogy of different menu choices when dining out. In the first scenario, you attend a reception with a plated meal, and the only offering is chicken (assuming no vegetarians are attending!). Unfortunately, the dish is a little overcooked and not seasoned particularly well. Perhaps you commiserate with your fellow diners. "Was your chicken dry?" you ask, wondering if everyone has the same opinion. But at the end of the night—outside of complaining and perhaps seeking a refund or a new entrée—you don't feel any culpability for a meal that fell below your expectations.

In the second scenario, the restaurant offers quite a large à la carte menu. Fish, beef, poultry, pasta . . . and multiple options for each! You order the chicken, which, as in our first example, turns out to be tough and bland. As other guests rave about their menu choices, you realize you chose poorly. ("Plate envy" is no fun.) Now you feel worse than in the single-item scenario; you feel somewhat responsible for the selection and perhaps even experience anger or resentment over the disparity.

For salespeople, a uniform plan is like the chicken in the first scenario: it might not be great, but at least everyone is in it together. PYOP options more resemble the second situation: if they don't work out as expected, many workers can't help wondering if they should have chosen differently. "Plan envy" can be demotivating.

One way to combat this type of buyer's remorse is to reduce the element of choice. PYOP approaches do not have to be limitless. Companies can also limit the number of performance metrics, where salespeople can claim that they would have done better under Option 1 versus Option 2. Rather, the PYOP element can center on the rewards—if you achieve the company's goals, you will get something you really want.

Potential inequity in the PYOP approach can be addressed by focusing on a single measurement with different reward mechanisms.

Each can be assigned points that take into account normalized dollars, risk profile, or nonmonetary value.

Complexity will undoubtedly increase with a PYOP approach, but new technologies with cloud-based analytics and Sales Performance Management (SPM) software will allow compensation administrators to manage multiple plan options simultaneously and tie formulas to individual reps with greater ease than ever before.

Sound far-fetched? The future may be closer than you think. BI Worldwide, a global leader in employee engagement, has already implemented a PYOP-type program, noting that people perform significantly better when self-selecting their goals. Called GoalQuest®, this program combines gamification and the motivational benefit of PYOP, allowing their clients' salespeople to select their own milestones: the larger the goal, the higher the payout when they meet or exceed expectations.

GoalQuest is protected by the U.S. Patent Office for its unique mix of self-selected goals, the all-or-nothing payout model, and its algorithmically escalating rewards. The methodology operates on these three simple pillars so that a salesperson is offered three goal levels above his or her current sales performance run rate. Once the reps select a goal level and commit to it, they cannot earn more by exceeding their selected goal, and they earn nothing if their performance falls shy of their selected goal. In other words, if the mid-level goal is selected, they cannot earn the bigger prize associated with the more aggressive goal even if their performance warrants it, because they will only earn at the goal level they've personally selected. Consequently, failing to reach their personally selected goal level results in no award at all. The methodology leverages goal ownership to keep people in the game: since they've chosen their own goal, it's their own and they're more committed to it than if it were assigned. And the program has proven to be a success, having been used with over one million participants across hundreds of Fortune 1000 organizations in 29 countries.

Although GoalQuest is typically deployed as a sales contest, technical improvements and software enhancements will soon enable companies to roll out similar, and more complex, programs as part of a base sales compensation package.

The key to maximizing motivation lies in creating plans that not only appeal to the salesperson's preferences (which will result in higher levels of drive) but also in structuring the rewards in a tiered manner. By combining these two elements, we can create plans and programs that offer incentives that people want, structured in a way to drive performance. Figure 3-9 shows a matrix Pick-Your-Own-Goal (a derivation of a Pick-Your-Own-Plan approach), which is built to appeal to a salesperson motivated by financial rewards. By offering rewards that matter with a clear linkage between those rewards and higher performance, we can incentivize the sales force to stretch and aim for overachievement.

Objectives \ Outcomes	$385,000	$423,000	$462,000	$500,000	$538,000	$577,000
$538,000	$1,620	$2,740	$4,200	$6,250	**$9,540**	$10,090
$500,000	$1,890	$3,220	$4,940	**$7,340**	$8,800	$10,000
$462,000	$2,230	$3,790	**$5,800**	$6,770	$8,120	$9,260
$423,000	$2,620	**$4,450**	$5,350	$6,250	$7,490	$8,540
$385,000	**$3,120**	$4,090	$4,920	$5,770	$6,910	$7,880

Figure 3-9. *Sample goal versus payout matrix in PYOP*

Looking Ahead

Like hula hoops, disco dancing, and pet rocks, fads can disappear. While one-size-fits-all comp plans won't completely vanish, we are confident more individualized plans will emerge. The money-centered comp programs of yesteryear will decline in popularity as comp plans that use a mix of reward mechanisms gain favor. Comp plans of tomorrow will be designed to resonate with an assortment of salespeople (including younger workers and an increasing number of women) who value money but are also inspired by noncash incentives, such as recognition, autonomy at work, and paid time off.

Comp plan managers can either embrace the changing workforce and employees' varied motivations or they can continue to develop one-size-fits-all plans that may fail to take into account individual motivational preferences. The potential consequence for stagnation: an engagement crisis with sales reps feeling deflated and discouraged because the comp plan offered to them isn't aligned with their motivations.

Managers and sales compensation professionals in the future will need to do two important things. First, they will need to understand the various underlying motivations in the sales force. Second, they will need to develop strategies to tap into those motivations to maximize the potential of the sales force. While it is possible that some companies discover that traditional cash-based incentives are sufficient to motivate their sales forces, all companies should develop plans that complement—not conflict with—employees' natural inspirations to achieve goals. They should not assume that all of their employees value money above all else. To help companies implement successful incentive programs in the future, suggested tactics can include:

- Conducting sales force interviews and surveys to capture sales reps' motivational preferences and better understand what types of rewards hold the most impact.
- Providing reward mechanisms and performance measurement options that align with preferred motivational drives. This can

include alternative ways of deploying the incentive program, such as gamification—which several well-regarded business journalists have reported as moving from hype to hip.

- Instituting new technologies and software to help alleviate the complexities associated with game design or multiple parallel comp plans. While the complexities of managing multiple plan options won't go away altogether, advances with cloud-based analytics and Sales Performance Management (SPM) software can make the administration easier.

Like the adoption of new technology, we do not expect every company to start implementing these practices immediately. Some may wish to kick-start their sales force or already recognize that their existing demographics lend themselves well to such changes. Others may try some of these tactics on a smaller scale, perhaps in short-term contests, to test the waters. And still others may take a wait-and-see approach or not feel the need for change based on the makeup of their sales organization. The end goal of any choice should be to ensure that the incentive program maximizes the motivation and impact of the sales organization.

CHAPTER 4

The Growth and Evolution of Sales Performance and Compensation Software

~

If Paul Revere had been a modern day citizen, he wouldn't have ridden down Main Street. He would have tweeted.

—Alec Ross

~

It is almost stunning to consider what technology did *not* exist 20 years ago (no Amazon, eBay, or Google). It is similarly hard to imagine that the iPhone only launched in 2007. Changes in technology are advancing at an accelerated and unprecedented pace. Many of the advances in hardware and software technology have been leveraged to improve sales compensation administration, and in the early 2000s, software specific to incentive compensation management began coming into its own. Incentive Compensation Management (ICM) software, like many other technologies, continues to evolve. As analysts and tech-savvy consumers alike eagerly await larger and higher definition TVs, next-generation smartphones, 3-D printing, and robotic appliances (such as the Roomba vacuum cleaning robot), sales compensation professionals are left to wonder: how will all this technological change affect the future of sales compensation?

In this chapter, we explore how ICM software and Sales Performance Management (SPM) software are likely to evolve over the next several years to take advantage of changes in hardware and software technology. Predicting changes in technology can be tricky (it wasn't that long ago that consumers were debating whether to buy an HD DVD or a Blu-ray player), but we can make some predictions based on analogous situations. Let's consider an analogy that may not be immediately obvious: the disappearance of the paper map industry.

How Technology Disrupted the Personal Navigation Industry

As a young child, I (Steve) often traveled 1,360 miles from Toronto, Canada, to Saint Petersburg, Florida, on family vacations. Along the drive, my brother and I would play "I Spy" and try to spot as many license plates as possible from different states and provinces. I recall being remarkably well behaved (although my parents might disagree), passing the remaining hours with my trusty Etch A Sketch (see Figure 4-1). Like many Boomer and Gen X kids, I got pretty creative with this basic drawing toy, where two knobs controlled an internal stylus that made impressions in an aluminum-oxide powder display.

Before the days of handheld video games, seat-back videos, and portable music players, my brother and I amused ourselves. The lack of technology also influenced the drive, which typically spanned several days.

"Is this our turn?" my mother would ask, as we tried to skirt around Pittsburgh.

"I don't know," Dad would reply. "Check the map."

Figure 4-1. *Etch A Sketch drawing toy*

Mom would pull a map out of the glove compartment, unfold it across half the dashboard and front seat, and squint at its tiny markings. Blue lines, black lines, bold lines. A bit of an art, map reading led to many heated debates between my parents. But to a child, figuring out the route was a puzzle, and getting lost was an adventure that culminated (finally!) in reaching our destination.

The Advent of Technology

Map reading has become almost completely unnecessary in today's world. Satellites now triangulate our locations and guide us via the Global Positioning System (GPS).

GPS devices date back to the 1960s for military use, but they went mainstream in the late 1990s when U.S. vice president Al Gore announced a plan to make GPS satellites transmit two additional signals to be used for civilian (nonmilitary) applications. By the end of the millennium, companies could overlay location data onto digital road maps, and brands like Garmin and TomTom had become household names. Early systems stored maps on the devices and charged fees to upgrade to newer versions. When Google entered this competitive arena with its Maps software on mobile phones, the paradigm changed and new features were introduced, including free and frequently updated maps, traffic reports, and eventually voice navigation for mobile phones.

As the competition in navigational software heated up, manufacturers sought ways to differentiate their products. Google Maps' watershed feature was a traffic tracker, which used Android-powered location data to display traffic flow and to provide estimated travel times based on actual congestion rather than simple travel distances—elements eventually replicated by the dedicated-device companies.

As the battle raged on, new, evolutionary entrants began to appear (see Figure 4-2). Apps like Waze (which Google later purchased in 2013 from an Israeli company for more than $1 billion) took the basic features—navigation and point-of-interest directions—from the previous generation of technologies and upgraded them by crowdsourcing real-time updates on accidents, police presence, red light cameras, and road closures (to name a few items). This new functionality allowed Waze to suggest alternate driving routes around traffic hot spots and identify the reason behind traffic slowdowns with an immediacy previously not available.

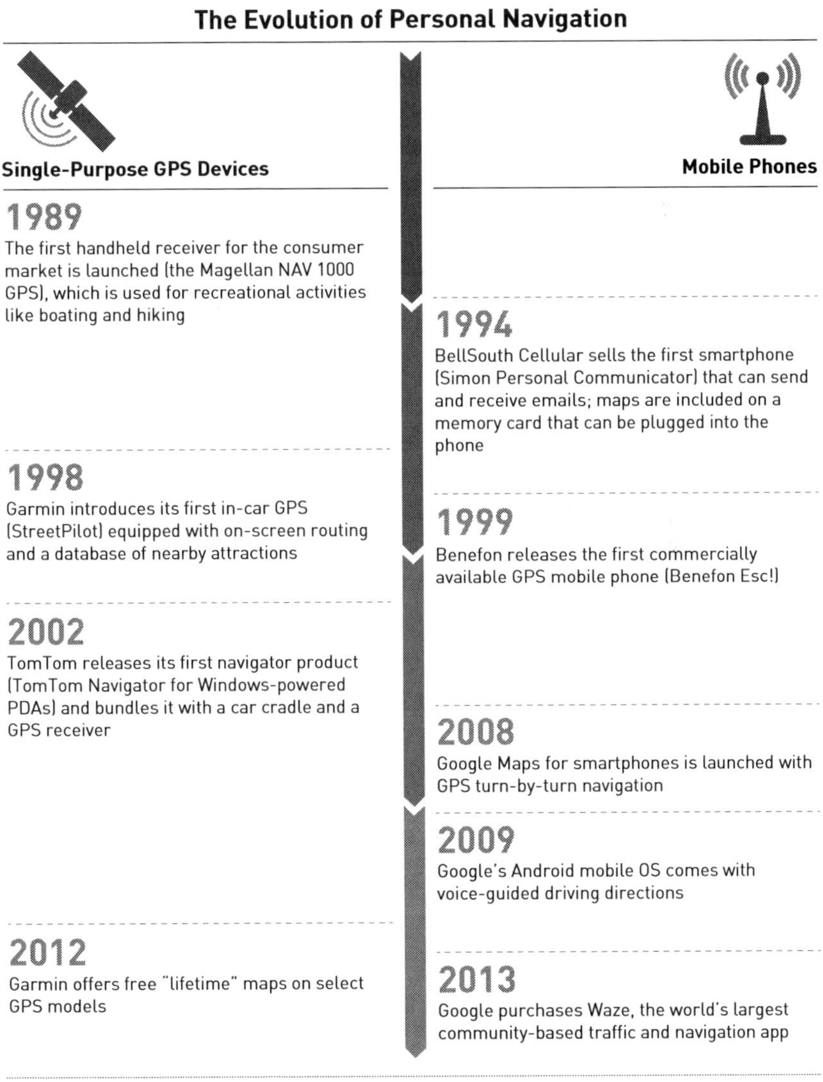

The Evolution of Personal Navigation

Single-Purpose GPS Devices

1989
The first handheld receiver for the consumer market is launched (the Magellan NAV 1000 GPS), which is used for recreational activities like boating and hiking

1998
Garmin introduces its first in-car GPS (StreetPilot) equipped with on-screen routing and a database of nearby attractions

2002
TomTom releases its first navigator product (TomTom Navigator for Windows-powered PDAs) and bundles it with a car cradle and a GPS receiver

2012
Garmin offers free "lifetime" maps on select GPS models

Mobile Phones

1994
BellSouth Cellular sells the first smartphone (Simon Personal Communicator) that can send and receive emails; maps are included on a memory card that can be plugged into the phone

1999
Benefon releases the first commercially available GPS mobile phone (Benefon Esc!)

2008
Google Maps for smartphones is launched with GPS turn-by-turn navigation

2009
Google's Android mobile OS comes with voice-guided driving directions

2013
Google purchases Waze, the world's largest community-based traffic and navigation app

Figure 4-2. *Moving in the right direction: A timeline of mapping technology*

Yes, the heyday of paper maps is long past. Technology has ushered in a new era of travel navigation. And sales compensation, like the personal-navigation industry, has been and will be impacted similarly by technological changes.

The Evolution of ICM and SPM Software

The rise of GPS and mobile phone navigation began with the realization that a new technology could be used to solve an existing problem. The problem with paper maps was not particularly earth-shattering, but it was one of convenience, efficiency, and safety. It was not efficient to have to stop the car (assuming you were traveling alone), pull out a paper map, locate your current position and destination, and write down (or memorize) your route. In sales compensation, a similar transformation took place. Technology—in the form of computers—became readily available, and the need to use this technology began to surface in the sales compensation area. What drove the need for computing power in sales compensation?

Consider the early salesperson, who sold widgets to other companies. Orders were placed, commissions were calculated, and checks were cut. The sales representative generally knew exactly how he or she was doing, thanks to a straightforward sales process and simple calculations of performance and commissions, often tallied with pens and paper ledgers. But the prevalence of a single-purpose salesperson with sole responsibility for sales is diminishing. Key and Strategic Account Managers, team selling, solution sales, inside sales, and channel or indirect sales are on the rise. As sales processes and sales compensation continue to grow more complex, technology offers new levels of quality and efficiency, particularly with PC-based calculations.

Technological advances enabled ever-more-complex equations to be processed, as well as enabling greater reporting functionality with graphs and charts created from the underlying data. And at some point, the commercial viability of a specific-purpose sales compensation product became clear.

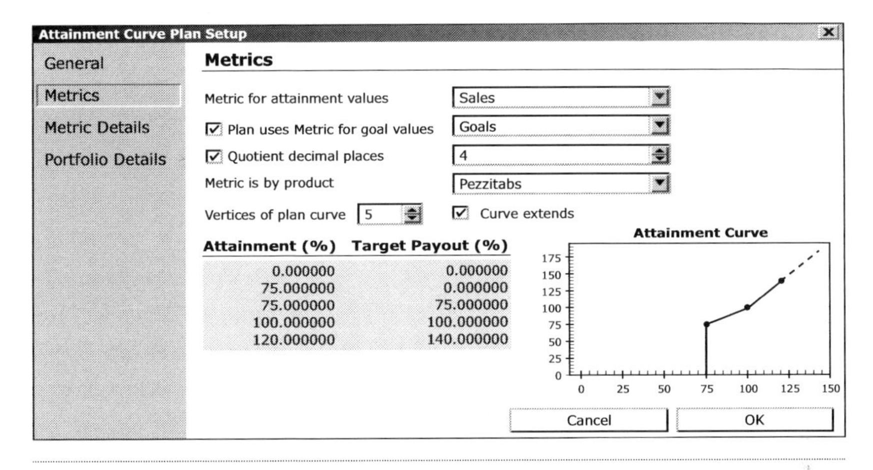

Figure 4-3. *ZS's early Prism ICM software's control panel*

One of the earliest ICM software solutions was brought to market by Trilogy, Inc. Founded in 1989, Trilogy was well known for its expertise in the insurance industry. Like many early ICM providers, Trilogy recognized the need for, and benefits of, a specific-purpose tool in a particular industry; ZS followed a similar approach when developing its early Olive and Prism ICM software, which evolved to Javelin SPM, for the healthcare industry (see Figure 4-3).

Over time, Trilogy evolved and, in early 2006, acquired Versata. With Versata, Trilogy offered insurance-specific and industry-neutral solutions, on-premise and Software-as-a-Service (SaaS) solutions, and continued to invest in product development amidst acquisitions and corporate reorganizations. During this time, other vendors entered the market for sales compensation software. Like Trilogy, these competitors refined and improved their ICM products, resulting in powerful and robust, yet flexible, programs that automated sales compensation.

Indeed, ICM software has disrupted the sales compensation administration process in much the same way that GPS devices shook up personal navigation. While people recognize that alternative options exist for ICM processing—most notably Microsoft office tools such as Excel or Access—those solutions are beginning to look more and more like paper maps: lower cost or basic options that may help you get to your end goal but that lack the high-tech features and functionality that will improve convenience, efficiency, and (in the case of comp) accuracy.

Recently, ICM software companies have started to take a more nuanced and holistic approach to sales compensation. Much like Waze built off of the basic mapping and navigation features of the early GPS devices and Google Maps, software providers are building off of the foundations of existing ICM software. Already, customers are looking for more than the specific-purpose ICM tools as they seek incremental value in adjacent areas like territory and quota management, coaching, and Management-By-Objectives (MBOs). As a result, ICM software is giving way to SPM software. SPM software offers a promise not unlike Waze's approach to navigation: to deliver a more integrated and valuable experience that goes above and beyond a single point solution. Around 2012, vendors started being evaluated on their overall SPM capabilities rather than solely on their ICM functionality. This approach was accompanied by a change in definition of "SPM" to include the following:

- Incentive compensation management
- Territory management
- Objectives and quota management
- Appraisal management
- Sales training management
- Hiring/onboarding management
- Coaching systems

Moving forward, how will technology shape our approach to sales compensation? And with the rise of SPM, will specific-purpose ICM tools become a thing of the past?

The changing landscape of technology and the rise of more integrated SPM solutions could doom existing ICM vendors in their current state, in much the same way that Waze and Google threatened the business viability of specific-purpose GPS navigation devices. Pure ICM vendors will generally need to follow one of three paths in the future:

- Remain a niche player and risk obsolescence (or position themselves for purchase)
- Expand their software offering, through either acquisition or development, into the broader SPM space
- Move into other, related areas to differentiate themselves from the competition

If current ICM vendors chose this third path, they would be following a strategy similar to that of Garmin, which could have easily folded under the competitive pressures in the personal navigation market. Instead, the Kansas-based multinational evolved its product line and moved into new areas, such as action cameras and GPS watches, appealing to a different base of customers. Existing ICM providers may need to reinvent themselves as new applications and more integrated SPM solutions come to market.

Xactly Corporation's CEO and founder, Chris Cabrera, and its COO and president, Evan Ellis, understand the competitive threat and the need to continuously evolve. Cabrera and Ellis see the future of ICM and SPM driven primarily by the growth of "big data." As more data becomes available—to organizations, to salespeople, and to customers—the ability to synthesize and draw actionable insights from ever-increasing volumes of data will help companies improve their sales compensation plans.

Xactly's data model for its SPM software is based on a true SaaS and cloud-based solution. By using standardized data formats, where each customer uses the same fields and naming conventions, and allowing customers to include their anonymized data in an aggregate database, Xactly can map and compare data across hundreds of thousands of salespeople. This is the basis for Xactly's Insights platform, which is essentially its "big data" crowdsourcing platform. (In Chapter 5, we explore the future of using data to create better compensation plans through analytics.) Ellis states the benefit of Insights succinctly: "It allows companies to unleash and unlock the data to make both tactical *and* strategic decisions."

How does this data enable more strategic decisions? Consider the use of advanced analytics in professional sports. Although *Moneyball*—the book and then the movie starring Brad Pitt about the early use of advanced analytics by the Oakland A's professional baseball team—brought analytics in sports to the attention of the general public, virtually every major professional sports league now has reams and reams of data available. For example, the National Basketball Association uses six SportVU cameras in each game to track player movement, capturing a wealth of data never before available, such as the distance players run, shooting positions, and assists. (What teams do with that data can certainly differ.)

Both SportVU and Insights are enabled through technology. Cabrera noted that even the data itself is a by-product of technology—technology that now allows for the capture and storage of increasing amounts of information. As a result of this information, organizations—be they sports teams or corporate entities—can make decisions and plot courses of action that were not possible before.

Cabrera points out one of the most exciting possibilities that this technological shift will enable: "The trend in the first years [of ICM] was really to automate. That was really the driving force behind these kinds of systems. But now, people are beginning to realize that the automation is the smallest piece of the ROI. The real ROI comes from getting your 5,000 salespeople to change their behavior. And it doesn't need to be a dramatic shift [to have a big impact]." The Insights service opens up real-time benchmarking, which allows sales leaders, human resources, and sales operations to compare—for example—their payouts to those of top performers in their industries. Such information can help sales comp practitioners and designers adjust parameters, plan metrics, and payout curves for maximum impact (see Figure 4-4). Whether through Insights or other platforms, expect big data to play an increasing role in helping sales compensation design to become more strategic and decisions to become more quantifiable in the near future.

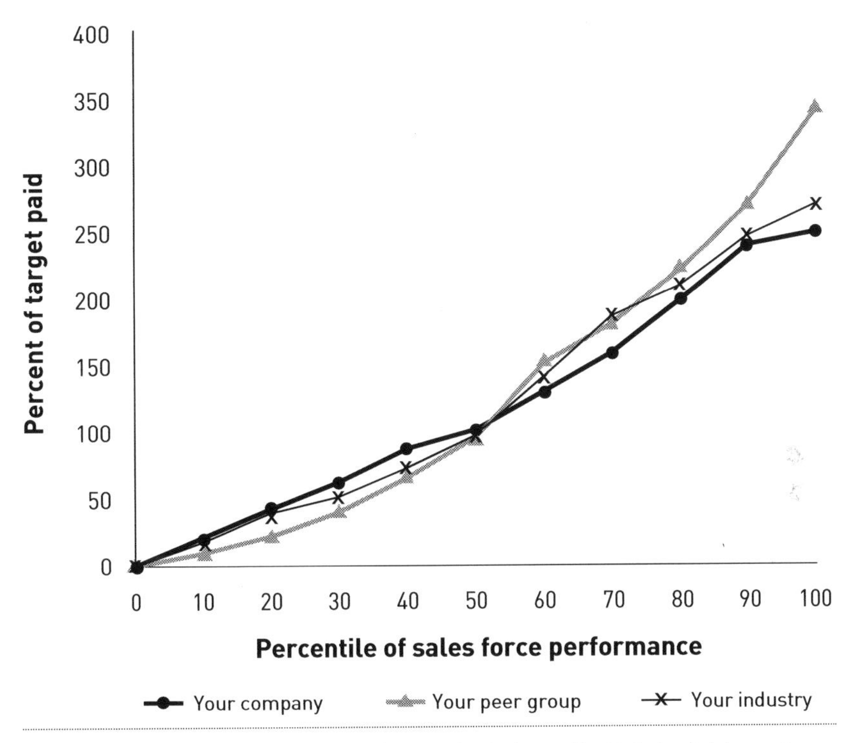

Figure 4-4. *Example of comparative analysis from Xactly's Insights system*

Another perspective on the future of SPM technology comes from Doug Smith, executive vice president and co-founder of Anaplan. Anaplan was designed as a cloud-based, flexible solution that provides visibility to large sets of data, open and rapid collaboration across users, and real-time updates to the data by those users. Founded in 2006, Anaplan has seen more than a 150% CAGR in the three-year period ending in 2015 with over $150MM in capital funding, reflecting the market excitement over its novel approach to software functionality. Anaplan's approach was not to build a specific ICM application (or, really, any specific-purpose application), but rather to deploy a platform that could adapt to and be configured for multiple functions. The Anaplan software therefore allowed unprecedented consistency across the entire SPM spectrum; companies can use Anaplan for multiple SPM use cases (such as territory and quota management, sales process planning, and forecasting) without having to license or learn multiple, disconnected single-purpose modules.

So what does the Anaplan approach and success to date suggest about changes in SPM software in the future? Smith notes that the existence of powerful, dynamic technology has accelerated by orders of magnitude in the last decade, which is obsoleting conventional technology. As a result, existing back-end point solutions (such as single-purpose ICM platforms) "don't perform well, don't scale, and don't help companies solve the problem they are truly trying to solve—the ability to optimize an integrated, holistic process that starts with targeting and ends with paying people the right amounts." And, Smith believes, "Challenges to Anaplan will not come from existing software applications, but from new entrants to the market built on yet-to-be-released technology."

One thing Cabrera, Ellis, and Smith have in common is a belief that data and technology are enabling their companies to succeed and differentiate themselves in the market. In the future, new technology and applications will flourish that allow compensation practitioners to make more strategic and timely decisions and build better plans through the use of improved descriptive, predictive, and prescriptive analytics. Such analytics—which we cover in more detail in Chapter 5—can be performed today, but they are often nonstandardized, can be difficult to design, and usually require manual intervention.

In addition to the increasing importance of software in the upstream, strategic planning phases of sales compensation, we expect three other trends to influence software design and usage in the future:

- The increasing demands of consumers for near real-time access to information
- The integration and evolution of gamification in sales comp programs and software
- The desire to customize compensation plans to maximize the motivational benefit to the sales force

Demands for Near Real-Time Access to Information

Millennial workers tend to have shorter attention spans than older workers, the result of the Information Age's instant access to all of human knowledge. Younger people don't want to wait, and have never really had to, when any question arises. But it's not just Millennials who have increasing demands for real-time information. As information becomes available more quickly, general consumers expect that they can get answers to their questions almost immediately. Comedian Pete Holmes summed up this phenomenon by stating, "The time between not knowing and knowing is so brief that knowing feels exactly like not knowing."

Holmes uses a humorous example of trying to find where Tom Petty was born. In the past, this investigation would have required talking to people, asking friends, and "impregnating [them] with wonder" such that they would help you find the answer. You would ask a friend, and if they didn't know, they would ask a friend. (The answer is Florida, in case you were wondering.) People have become so accustomed to instant access to information that any delay feels unacceptable. Data back up Holmes's perspective. More than 3.5 billion searches are run on Google daily. If Google's answers roll out even 0.4 seconds more slowly, it reduces the number of searches by millions per day. In fact, a quarter of cybersurfers abandon web pages that take more than four seconds to load, and half of mobile users bail at 10 seconds (apparently we are more tolerant of delays on our mobile phones). Indeed, our desire for instant gratification will (and is already beginning to) spill into the sales compensation space.

As Chris Cabrera notes, "[Smartphones] are the modern-day 'dangling carrot.' The way to affect behaviors and the way to a salesperson's mind now is through these devices. We didn't have that technology before."

Incentive plan designs will need to change to accommodate our escalating impatience, and ICM software will need to adapt as well. It no longer will take weeks (or months) to process data, calculate performance, report information, and pay workers. Parallel and in-memory processing will drive near real-time updates, allowing SPM software to better motivate and engage the sales force. Yes, technology will need to be dynamic and visually interesting, but it will also need to be fast for sales compensation purposes, just as it has become fast to support our increasing appetite for data in less and less time (see Figure 4-5). Successful software vendors in the future will be those that offer in-the-cloud solutions, in-memory processing, and end-to-end truly integrated functionality that limits data transfers or external handling. (Many of today's SPM vendors have numerous modules that enable holistic SPM functionality; however, these modules were often bought and "tacked on" to the solution to sell a vision of end-to-end functionality. Many an unsuspecting buyer came to realize that these modules don't actually speak to one another in a seamless manner.)

The Technological Gamification of Compensation Plans

As discussed in Chapter 3, expect more playfulness and the increasing gamification of sales compensation. Gamification will likely assume a new name, as companies experience "gamification fatigue" and vendors seek to differentiate themselves. Regardless of its name, software will need to evolve to truly handle gamification and gameful design in a way that maximizes effectiveness.

Also addressed in Chapter 3 is that many current gamification software programs are little more than simple themes—golf, basketball, racing cars—layered on top of rankings. Simple games can be deployed in hours using existing software: select a metric, pick your theme, pipe that metric into the game system, and rank salespeople based on their performance on that measure. Sales results, call activity, leads generated, opportunities closed—if it's in your CRM system, it can probably be linked to a game. Yet true gamification, using the principles of game theory in non-game situations, is not supported today in a robust way. Part of the reason is that technology providers have not focused on game design (in much the same way that most current technology providers have not focused on sales compensation design).

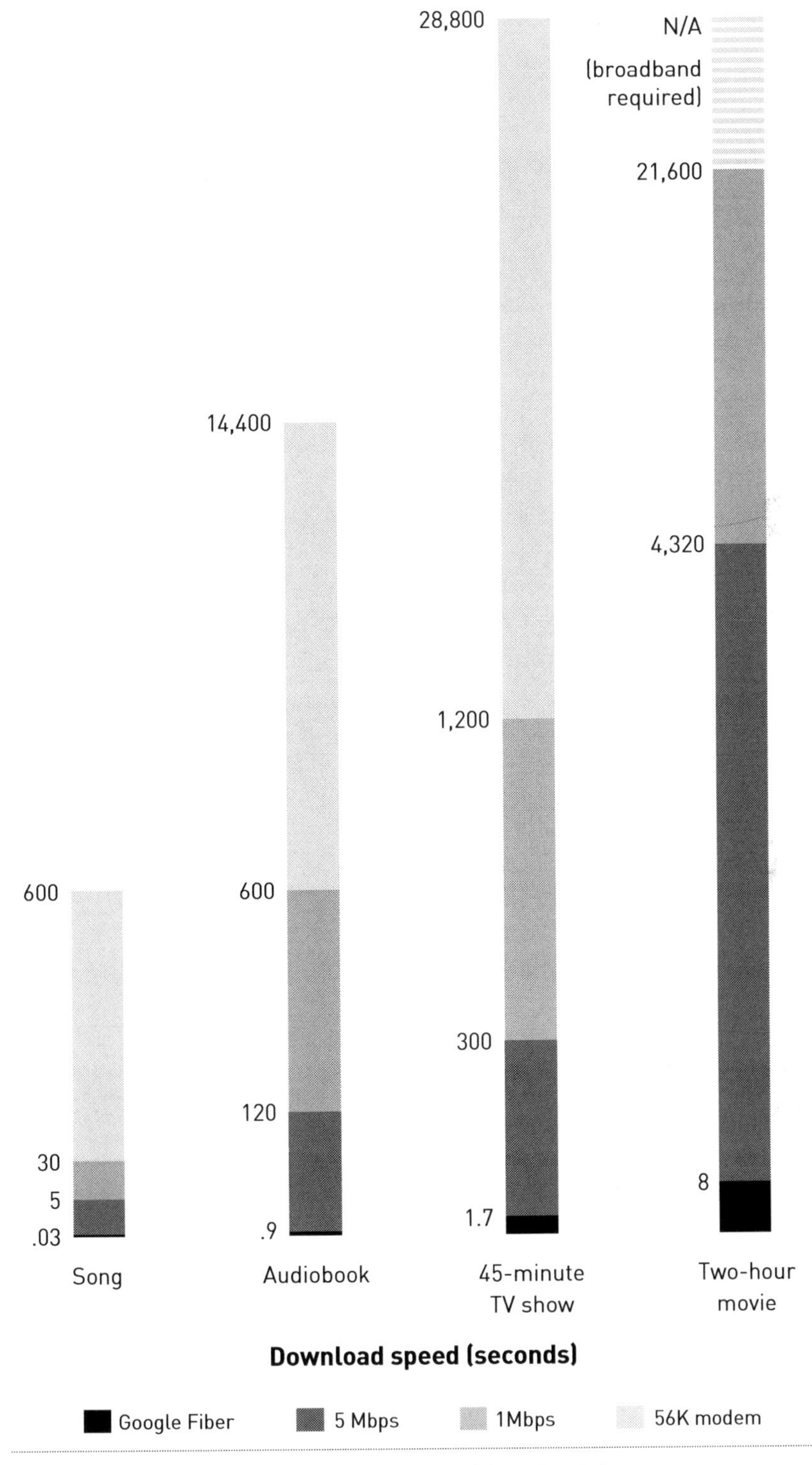

Figure 4-5. *The need for speed: A history of download times*

Technology today is used to track and report salespeople's progress, but sales instructions and directions often come from sales leaders, email blasts, and Brainsharks. What is the purpose of these communications? Often, to provide guidance and direction to the sales force. In the future, some of this can instead come through the games themselves. Although the creative design of effective games will likely continue to happen outside of the software, technology can help improve the efficiency and effectiveness of gamification and game design in sales comp. We expect this will take two forms. First, gamification software will support the design of better games by providing frameworks and "prebuilt" games. Much like Xactly's Insights provides real-time benchmarking to aid in the design of compensation plans, prepackaged game options will provide companies with game options from which they can choose.

Second, as technology allows for the development of custom apps in increasingly shorter periods of time, companies will no longer be limited to basic games, like stack-ranked competitions with fancy wrappers. Rather, the introduction of custom apps will enable the creation of more robust games to engage the sales force. Software will enable designers to build and deploy true games that will, in many cases, be accessed through a smartphone, thereby providing near real-time direction and updates while keeping required or desired activities at the tips of the sales force's fingers.

Managing the Increased Personalization of Compensation Plans

As we talked about in Chapter 3, the demands of Millennials and "pick your own plan" incentives—designed to maximize motivation—will lead to increasing levels of personalization in sales compensation. Technology and software will play a critical role in enabling and encouraging these types of plans. Without the enabling technology, the administrative complexity and burden of personalized plans will be too heavy to be practical. Sales operations teams today often struggle with administering plans with numerous exceptions—and exceptions are essentially a series of minor personalizations. Administrators often cite the difficulty in managing plans with a large number of exceptions and push their design counterparts to simplify and consolidate the plans. But these challenges should, in part, be handled through more flexible and powerful technology. Software will be developed that enables the necessary flexibility to handle personalizations, and high-speed processing hardware will ensure that system operations do not bog down with increasing complexity. We are seeing the early phases of this shift today.

One company has already created specific-purpose software that enables and measures a type of plan personalization. BI Worldwide offers a software application called GoalQuest, which we covered in more detail in Chapter 3. GoalQuest enables companies to deploy a contest where reps pick their own goal from a predetermined and limited subset of options; the higher the goal you pick, the greater the reward if you reach that goal. Higher goal, higher reward; lower goal, lower reward. Intuitively, the idea makes sense to everyone with whom we speak: salesperson motivation will be maximized when they "own" their objectives, and applications like GoalQuest help both maximize motivation and avoid "sandbagging"—the practice of underestimating your ability to sell in order to get a lower goal. While sandbagging can still occur with GoalQuest, a strong financial disincentive discourages the practice. GoalQuest is typically deployed only in contests, but during our project work at ZS, we have discussed the idea of personalized plans as part of the standard sales compensation program with many organizations. One of the main challenges with a broader deployment of personalized plans remains the technical feasibility more so than the perceived value.

To enable the personalization of sales compensation plans, we'll need higher-speed processing and larger data-handling capabilities, along with software designed for maximum flexibility. Much of this is already happening organically, as technology designers push the boundaries of performance. However, when it comes to evolution and release of new SPM software, we believe three technological changes will need to occur before the personalization of compensation plans becomes more prevalent:

- SPM software vendors will need to take advantage of technological advancements in hardware that will enable faster and more powerful processing.
- The current rigid software architecture of many of today's SPM platforms will need to be made more flexible, so that what we now call an "exception" becomes part of an easily managed norm.
- More advanced plan modeling capabilities will be needed that allow companies to understand the implication of various combinations of personalized plan options.

We can touch on each of these in detail.

1. New hardware technologies are rarely—if ever—developed solely with sales compensation in mind. Developing technology that will "create a market" is seldom successful (unless your company logo looks like a piece of fruit with a bite taken out of the side). Therefore, as technology advances, sales compensation applications will need to be created that leverage the ever-increasing processing capabilities and speed of new hardware. Further, as ICM platforms evolve, industry leaders will create more flexible and adaptable platforms that allow sales compensation administrators to build more complex and personalized compensation programs.
2. Creating ICM software to handle the flexibility and complexity of personalized incentive plans will not be straightforward. Many of today's commercial sales compensation applications anchor around a paradigm of "one plan per role." Given the challenges that some current ICM software have when dealing with even a limited number of exceptions, an evolution to a plan design that allows for "custom incentive elements per person" could be significant. Companies that build this flexibility into their software will have an advantage in the future.
3. The analytics performed by companies and the capability of compensation software has to improve dramatically when using

personalized plans. Why? When modeling traditional incentive plans, many companies use techniques such as Monte Carlo simulations (a problem-solving technique used to approximate the probability of certain outcomes by running multiple simulations) to estimate the performance distributions and resulting payouts. However, when personalized plans are in place, these modeling techniques will be insufficient. As personalized incentive plans may have different objectives or rewards, modeling these plans will require more complex multivariate analyses. When traditional modeling tools (typically Excel) become unable to handle these complex analytics, companies will turn to software to streamline the modeling. Modeling and predicting outcomes will become a more important part of the software's feature set as a result of personalized plans.

As Cabrera, Ellis, and Smith describe their visions for the future of the sales compensation space, one thing is clear: while the path forward can and will differ by vendor, both software and technology will continue to play significant roles in the future of sales compensation.

Looking Ahead

This is probably the easiest—or maybe it's the hardest?—chapter for us to provide short-term action items because many of our predictions are based on changes to technology that are yet to happen. However, we can offer up a few short-term alternatives. Keep in mind that technology is an enabler. Before Henry Ford produced the Model T automobile, it wasn't as though cars didn't exist; he was the first to mass-produce the "horseless carriage." Similarly, technology will make available things to the masses that, with some hard work (manual processes) or technical workarounds, you can begin to realize now.

Here are four ways you can get ahead of today's technical limitations:

1. **Start small.** Most companies are rather conservative when it comes to investments in radical changes to sales force compensation. They don't plunge headlong into the deep end; instead,

they wade into the pool gradually. The pace of technological changes may prevent us from jumping in at the deep end, so we might need to dip a toe. Try new technologies in limited situations. A good vehicle for testing new technologies is the sales contest. Look for situations where you can try processes or test tools with pilot groups without disrupting the entire sales force.

2. **Leverage existing software as your starting point.** While current technology might not be perfect for the purposes we describe in this chapter, that doesn't mean you can't use it at all. For example, most current ICM applications offer users the ability to copy and model new plan design options. You can certainly create a complex modeling scenario in a sandbox environment with multiple plan options combined to create something akin to a personalized plan. Additionally, many software vendors will be willing to deploy a proof of concept in a limited engagement to demonstrate that the software or process works. If so, you may feel more comfortable making a purchasing commitment; if the software doesn't support your desired process, every software vendor is looking for feedback for product enhancements.
3. **Don't be afraid of manual processes.** In cases where the software may not fulfill all of your requirements (and that will probably be most cases in the beginning), don't be afraid to use manual processes. While Excel wasn't designed for complex modeling, if existing software cannot handle some of your requirements, Excel may be a viable alternative to create models that are flexible enough to measure and track performance. Once you have a working model, you can begin to optimize and automate it.
4. **Include specs related to your future vision now.** Many current SPM vendor evaluations use boilerplates to capture your compensation administration requirements. Consider your future vision and include your "wish list" features—things that you would love to have in the software in five years—as part of your current evaluation. Your "future wish list" may shape your present-day technology choices; don't pick software that will limit you in a few years.

As SPM software evolves, it is difficult to predict what changes are truly coming. What we do know is that the future of sales compensation technology will be exciting!

CHAPTER 5

Taking Your Sales Compensation Analytics to the Next Level

~

In God we trust, all others bring data.

—W. Edwards Deming

~

Remember that sinking feeling of being sent to the principal's office when you were a kid? Your face felt hot. There was a queasy sensation in the pit of your stomach, a sense that something really bad was about to happen. As you were escorted down the school's hallway, your teacher read you your last rites and your fellow students waved as if to say good-bye. Well, maybe it wasn't that grim, but it sure didn't feel nice to have to meet with the principal.

Fast-forward 15, 20, or 30 years, and you are now in the business world, managing your own team, in a successful career. But even as an adult, you aren't immune to uncomfortable meetings with your superiors.

To illustrate this point, here's a story that might sound familiar: Marc Schoenen is Google's compensation director. It's a high-ranking position with a lot of responsibility. One afternoon Schoenen is asked to meet with the company's chief financial officer. (Here comes that queasy feeling.) Though unaware of the meeting's agenda, Schoenen knows from experience that this isn't going to be a pleasant conversation. When the leader of a company's sales compensation program is invited to speak with the Finance department, most likely something unexpected has happened with the sales compensation spend. Knowing this, Schoenen walks to the CFO's office ready for a tense exchange.

But what if Schoenen could avoid these types of visits with Finance altogether? Or better yet, what if he had utilized predictive analytics and could proactively go to the CFO with his concerns *and* recommended solutions?

Changing the Conversation

In the past, and even now, the role of analytics in sales compensation has been mostly descriptive or "backward looking"—assessing a plan's pay-for-performance relationship, reviewing payout statistics, and so on. In fact, our experience suggests that descriptive analytics make up over 80 percent of the analytics done today. This type of information is useful for tracking performance and telling you how your comp plan has been working historically. But what if Finance asks you to predict how your plan *will* perform? What data could you provide? Probably not much if you are using only descriptive analytics and no predictive analytics, and being empty-handed is only going to make the conversation with your CFO more stressful.

Introducing Predictive Analytics to Your Organization

Predictive analytics is the practice of data mining historical and current information to make future predictions. These analytics are probably already part of your daily life:

- **Netflix** tells you which movies you're likely to enjoy based on past selections and how you rated them.
- **LinkedIn** predicts which business contacts you should connect with.
- **Amazon** makes recommendations based on your purchase history and the purchase history most similar to you.
- **Spotify** keeps a running tab of your likes and dislikes to create the perfect music list.

Predictive analytics in sales compensation, the practice of extracting information from data and using it to predict pay and performance trends, can give you the foresight you need. It will help you change the conversation with Finance, and with everyone else, for the better.

For Schoenen and other compensation leaders, predictive analytics are critical for proactive sales compensation management. Why? Because descriptive analytics tell a company what just happened, but predictive analytics do something even more important: they tell leaders what is likely to happen and help to kick-start the process of generating solutions to solve future comp plan problems.

In the Beginning: Descriptive Analytics

Because predictive analytics usually build off of descriptive analytics, let's start with a very brief overview of what we mean by "descriptive analytics."

As we have discussed, descriptive analytics focus on what has happened in the past. They rarely look to the future but instead provide key company stakeholders (VPs Sales, CEOs, CFOs, and so on) with dashboards and reports.

Descriptive analytics are most certainly useful in sales compensation. They provide an assessment of how the incentive plan and supporting administration processes performed. They also help monitor performance on key metrics against defined "target zones." These target zones may come from externally sourced benchmarks, industry standards, previous results, or financial standards that are important to the company. Examples of target zones are listed in Figure 5-1.

	Category and Metrics	Target
Payouts	Percent of the sales team at or above quota	50–60%
	Percent of the sales team with >$0 payout	90–100%
	Percent of the team with ≥75% of target payout	60–80%
	Ratio of payout at 10th percentile to target pay	0.1X–0.3X
	Ratio of payout at 90th percentile to target pay	2X–3X
	SPIFFs as a percent of actual incentive	3–7%

Figure 5-1. *Benchmark payout statistics*

But even the best descriptive analytics can only say where a company is (or was) at a specific point in time. Few actually attempt to predict where a company will be at a point in the future, a far more useful bit of information—and much more actionable.

Predicting the Future

By using predictive analytics, we can accurately predict what will happen at the end of a performance period and proactively act on those findings. This isn't to imply that companies aren't already using predictive analytics. One of the most common predictive analytics tools is used currently to estimate the costs of newly designed sales incentive plans. This includes predicting what the plan will cost in aggregate at multiple performance levels, how individual salespeople will be affected, and so on. For example, Monte Carlo simulations can help companies understand the range of costs under many different performance scenarios.

But this use of predictive analytics is the exception. We have seen time and time again companies not using predictive analytics, thus missing out on opportunities to understand how a plan is likely to perform, whether the plan will deliver the desired results, and whether intervention is needed. We think that's going to change, though.

The future of sales compensation will largely build on the ample amount of descriptive analytics currently used and will improve on them by making them more predictive. By effectively using predictive analytics, sales comp leaders can successfully intervene and provide recommendations that could avoid or minimize significant issues, including comp plan cost overruns, salesperson resignations, and a demotivated sales force.

Specifically, we believe that companies will increase their use of predictive analytics in these areas (at a minimum):

- Turnover reduction
- Midcourse corrections
- Field inquiries

Turnover Reduction

In the last several years, several companies have made headlines with their efforts to predict which employees may leave and what actions managers can take to reduce turnover. For example, in the book *Predictive Analytics: The Power to Predict Who Will Click, Buy, Lie, or Die*, Eric Siegel, a former assistant professor of computer science at Columbia University, discusses Hewlett-Packard's (HP) Flight Risk program. The program was designed to predict employee resignations based on a variety of factors such as career opportunities, work tasks, leadership, and compensation. According to Siegel, by identifying likely attrition and taking preventive action, HP was able to reduce employee turnover from 20 percent to 15 percent in a pilot group. It is reported that these findings led HP to forecast that a company-wide implementation of the program could result in $300 million in potential savings.

Similarly, other organizations have successfully used turnover predictions to reduce staff resignations. Credit Suisse found that by opening up more jobs for internal consideration, employee retention improved. After revamping the internal job postings process, about 300 people were promoted, many of whom would have been at risk for resignation. Credit Suisse has estimated that a reduction in turnover of a single point will save $75 million to $100 million annually.

The predictive models in these examples are for all employees (at least based on what was reported in the media). We believe that if these turnover prediction models were created for salespeople, companies may find slightly different factors driving turnover. Specifically, we believe sales compensation would come up as one of the predictors of turnover, even though it was not mentioned as a factor in the case studies discussed above.

Why? Our experience and research have shown that salespeople are more likely than employees in other roles to name compensation as one of the factors that cause turnover, likely due to the much higher portion of their total compensation at risk. (If incentive compensation is done poorly, it has a much greater impact on the salesperson's take-home pay and job satisfaction.)

Companies know this intuitively, but they have to take it to the next level. Companies must take advantage of the advent of predictive analytics and develop predictive turnover models that assess salesperson likelihood to leave.

This is important because the cost of losing a salesperson is significantly higher than that of other staff. The Society for Human Resources Management estimates it costs $3,341 to replace a traditional employee. But the cost (including opportunity costs) of losing a productive salesperson goes significantly beyond this number: estimates have been between $50,000 and $1 million depending on the company. (See Figure 5-2.)

What causes such a huge discrepancy in employee turnover costs between sales and non-sales? Salespeople are profit centers, pure and simple. Each salesperson generates a certain amount of revenue annually for his or her organization. When a top salesperson begins to look for other employment opportunities, it triggers a very expensive chain reaction that reduces revenue and increases costs:

- Salesperson productivity wanes as the person takes time to search for a new job and loses focus on (and motivation for) his or her current role.

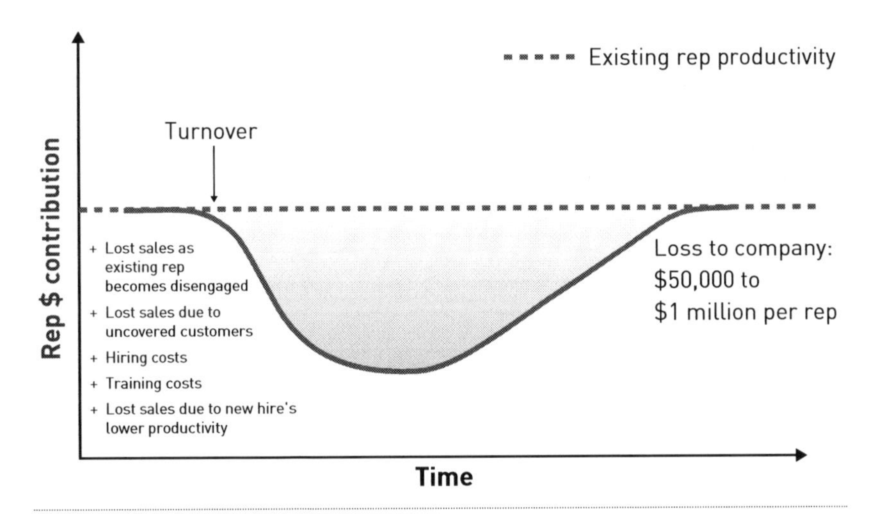

Figure 5-2. *Cost of sales rep turnover*

- Once the salesperson quits, the sales territory may remain vacant for months, leading to lost revenue due to noncoverage or reduced coverage.
- When the new sales rep is identified, the company incurs hiring and training costs and also compensation "guarantees" while the person is being onboarded.
- Finally, it will take the new salesperson time to reach the revenue productivity level of the departing sales rep—anywhere from a few months to a few years. The difference in productivity between the departing sales rep and the replacement should be included in the cost of turnover.

All of these costs and lost revenues add up to significant dollars, making employee attrition much more expensive for the sales role.

Not only are salespeople one of the most costly staff positions when it comes to turnover expenses, but they are also the most likely to resign or be let go. The U.S. Bureau of Labor Statistics published a list showing the median job tenure of selected occupations, and the sales role had the lowest longevity (see Figure 5-3).

US Foods knows the high potential for sales staff resignations, and that's why the company is segmenting out its strongest performers, giving them incentives to stay. These can include guarantees on their commissions and off-cycle increases in their salaries. "We are making sure we put a packet in front of them that shows we care," says Brian Sinclair, senior director of compensation at US Foods. "If security is the issue, let's think about guarantees or retention-type devices. If it is about paying them competitively, we will fix that too."

When you combine the extreme costs of sales rep departures with the high amount of turnover, any improvement that lowers employee loss will have a significant impact on a company's top and bottom lines. Because of these findings, we believe that there is a place for sales organizations to utilize compensation information (along with other engagement factors) to start predicting the likelihood that sales team members will leave the company. And we aren't the only ones who think so.

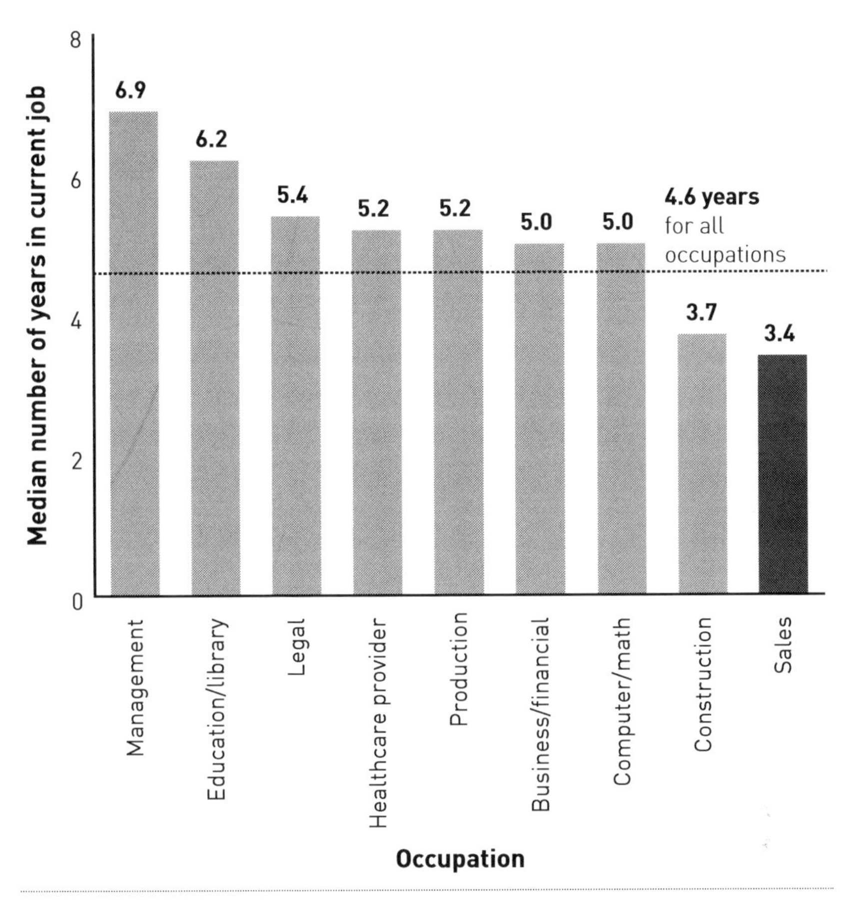

Figure 5-3. *Median job tenure of selected occupations, 2014*
Source: U.S. Bureau of Labor Statistics.

During a sales compensation conference session on predictive analytics, we asked participants, "What is something you are most likely to take back to your organization as a result of what you learned in this session?" The number one answer: We must find a way to reduce regrettable salesperson turnover using predictive analytics.

Best-in-class companies will create models that predict the likelihood that individual salespeople will leave. They will then use that information to predict who is most likely to resign and will take proactive steps to reduce the turnover rate, particularly among top performers.

Companies with a limited budget can do a simple correlation using available data to begin to predict the probability that particular salespeople will quit. Ideally, this would include hard quantifiable data (percent to quota, payouts, performance review score) combined with some type of survey data gauging their perceptions on multiple aspects known to affect salesperson retention and engagement.

If your firm already conducts a regular engagement survey for your employees, you could easily leverage that survey to do an assessment of salesperson turnover. Your engagement survey administrator should be able to separate out the sales function and conduct a separate engagement analysis for this job role. The administrator may be able to do an additional analysis that narrows the engagement outcomes to just the retention/turnover question scores. This would make the turnover analysis even more accurate, as the employment factors would be predicting just turnover, not the broader engagement measure.

Midcourse Corrections

Many organizations regularly track descriptive statistics that look backward—such as the percentage of reps at quota, how much has been paid in incentives thus far, and so on. But few organizations are good at predicting where their sales forces will end up at the end of the year, and as a result, they end up missing out on the benefits of midcourse corrections.

Here's an example. A paper sales company in New Jersey has just finished Q2 payouts and reporting, and the sales force is at 84 percent of its year-to-date quota. What should be done about it? In a descriptive statistics scenario, the company only knows where it has been. It could make a simplifying assumption and assume that the sales force will end the year at 84 percent of quota unless some intervention is taken. And the company might be right. However, predictive analytics would allow companies to make a more accurate assessment.

Most companies that find themselves in scenarios like this are not sure what to do. They may try to solve the problem by implementing disparate tactics, such as short-term SPIFFs, or they may even consider lowering the quotas. But that begins to look like desperation to the sales team, and they sense there is a problem—with the products they're selling, the quotas they were given, or perhaps even the sales force itself. And it also begins to condition the sales force to expect a bailout as soon as results start going south.

What companies can do is get better at predicting where they truly will be at the end of the year and, if intervention is needed, which form of intervention would be most effective. For example, with the paper company's sales force at 84 percent of quota, the best practice is to forecast where the sales force will be at year's end and take appropriate action based on the root causes. Tactics could include using seasonality trends and pipeline information. It is entirely possible that Q2 was lower than historical seasonality and that the pipeline is stronger than it typically is at that time of year. In this case, a midyear correction would not be advised.

However, it also could be that sales performance in Q2 is the beginning of a downward trend, indicating that the organization is heading for an even worse fate by the end of the year. In that case, a serious intervention is required. Again, data on seasonality, business trends, and pipeline can help make that determination.

In Figure 5-4, the examples of common descriptive statistics that companies have tracked could be transformed into prescriptive statistics, allowing for better midcourse corrections.

Descriptive Statistic	Predictive Statistic	Potential Action
32% of reps are hitting YTD quota through June	37% of reps will hit their full-year quota	Consider partial quota reduction that will bring 43% of reps up to 100% of quota
Sales force achieved 109% of budget through June	Full-year performance will be 111%	Accrue additional funds now for the full-year incentive plan payouts
Pay levels have fallen 14% below market	Turnover will increase by 5 percentage points	Move high performers to market pay levels immediately, and move medium performers to within 10% of market

Figure 5-4. *Moving from descriptive statistics to predictive statistics to potential actions*

Field Inquiries

We've discussed two areas where companies will increasingly use predictive analytics: staff turnover reduction and midcourse corrections. Now, let's look at the third area: field inquiries.

While administering sales compensation for a Fortune 100 healthcare company, ZS received several calls every month from salespeople who had questions about their reported performance, sales force rank, and associated payout calculation.

As the questions came in, we would look up the individual's information and their rank change. We would then research the change in the individual's calculations that comprise their performance and payout, and compare this to the change in the overall sales force performance. The research could take several days, depending on the question.

In reviewing which salespeople were calling ZS and why, we noticed that the most common cause was a significant shift in sales force rank: people who had dropped more than a certain number of places were highly likely to phone ZS. In response to this correlation, we began automatically generating a detailed analysis of why anyone over a certain downward rank change threshold was dropping in the ranking.

We set up an automated process to replicate the thought process that an analyst would go through. For individuals calling us after the monthly reports were issued, the average wait time to let them know why their rank dropped went from a few days to a few hours. The takeaway: companies that anticipate questions from specific people in the field will cut down manual work (and costs) and increase customer satisfaction with the sales organization.

Companies can shorten the time the field has to wait for ad hoc analyses by predicting who will call in, and why, and run these ad hoc analyses automatically when the performance reports are produced. There may be obvious areas that deserve attention and an automatic analysis—people who drop more than a certain percentage of quota or anyone who has a negative sales credit appear, for example. There may be other areas that you uncover in analyzing your own experience with the field. This is the type of predictive analytics that allows you to be proactive with the sales force and add significant value.

Moving from Prediction to Action

While predictive analytics are the future for sales compensation, incentive leaders can add even more value for company leaders by offering a recommended solution based on the predictions. Data are used to drive predictions, but the guiding principles of the company's sales compensation program can be combined with those predictions to turn them into action.

For example, say a company conducts predictive analytics estimating that only 30 percent of salespeople are going to hit their quota at the end of the year. (As Figure 5-1 noted, this percentage should be in the 50 to 60 percent range.) That prediction may elicit very different responses based on the company's culture and the principles with which it governs its sales incentive plan. One company might have a policy that makes quota adjustments virtually impossible. It believes that quota adjustments this year lead to setting that expectation in future years and damage the credibility of the sales leadership team. In this type of culture, the right "prescription" may be to do nothing.

But another company might have a culture that is more forgiving. For example, it might have a policy that if 40 percent of salespeople miss their quota, it's the individual salespeople who have failed, but if 70 percent miss their quota, it's likely a problem with the quota. In this environment, a projection that only 30 percent will hit their goals would likely lead to a midyear quota adjustment.

Similarly, many companies conduct financial modeling when designing the sales incentive plan for the following year. Financial modeling reveals the most likely pay and performance distribution of the new plan. If the initial plan modeling shows that nobody would earn $0 and the 10th percentile earners would get 50 percent of their target incentive, the company's response depends a lot on the culture and the guiding principles that drive incentive plan design.

How does this relate to you? If your company skews toward a very strong pay-for-performance culture, you likely will raise the minimum performance threshold prior to rolling out the new plan such that some sales reps would be out of the money. You may also lower the payment earned at threshold so that bottom performers earn less. Making these changes would allow you to increase the payout for top performers, while keeping the overall payout the same, allowing you to reflect the desired pay-for-performance message.

However, if your company is more team-oriented and less focused on pay-for-performance, the results from the financial modeling might be just fine. It might be that you have a selling process that involves a lot of different team members, thus making it very difficult to determine which sales rep or reps actually influenced a particular sale. In these circumstances, you may choose to leave the minimum performance threshold and the payout at threshold as they are. The company culture and inability to determine causality may lead to lower payout differentiation.

Looking Ahead

More data have been generated in the last two years than in the prior million years combined. Predictive analytics are all around us. A new college major called Data Science has been created to help make sense of all the data. We believe that analytic advances will be applied to sales compensation data in the near future. In this chapter, we highlighted some of the areas where predictive analytics can be applied to sales compensation, such as:

1. Reducing sales rep turnover, which in turn saves a company up to $1 million for each salesperson retained who would have left
2. Predicting how the sales comp plan is likely to perform in the future and using the predictions to potentially suggest midyear corrections
3. Identifying outliers on sales performance and proactively determining why they are outliers

Many companies have developed robust descriptive analytics when it comes to sales compensation, but telling executives, CFOs, and sales leaders "how it was" is no longer good enough. Best-in-class sales compensation and sales operations groups are using predictive analytics to help determine future payouts and performance; to identify salespeople who are at risk for leaving; and to anticipate and head off questions from the field. The result is that predictive analytics will add an enormous amount of value to company leadership by enabling proactive action that will increase sales performance and morale and reduce sales rep turnover. And they might just allow you to make any visit to the CFO's office much more pleasant and predictable.

CHAPTER 6

Getting Your Sales Force to Embrace a New Sales Comp Plan

~

It is not the strongest of the species that survives,
nor the most intelligent that survives. It is the one
that is the most adaptable to change.

—Charles Darwin

~

Samantha Harris, vice president of sales operations for a large financial services firm, couldn't believe the feedback she was getting on the sales incentive plan she had rolled out last year. The responses collected from the sales force through a survey revealed that only 37 percent of sales reps could accurately describe how the sales compensation plan worked. Interviews with the senior vice president of sales and the company's chief finance officer disclosed their belief that the plan was not driving the business results they were seeking. As the person ultimately responsible for the design and administration of the sales incentive plan, Harris was very concerned about the way the incentive plan was playing itself out and whether the company's goals would be achieved. She was also understandably worried about keeping her job.

How did Harris find herself in this position? She knew the stakes were high when she led the design process at the end of last year. She had brought in external benchmarking to help her design the plan and ensure she wasn't limiting her thinking to her own experiences. She had interviewed the company's senior executives about their strategy for driving growth within the sales organization. Her team had modeled the plan to ensure that the sales organization would hit appropriate pay-for-performance benchmarks. But it wasn't working: the salespeople didn't understand the plan, and it wasn't bringing the company the desired results.

Many sales compensation leaders can relate to Harris's story. Time and time again we hear from our clients about their experiences rolling out new comp plans that failed to motivate their sales forces. In this chapter, we will explore ways to successfully launch major plan designs that will resonate with salespeople *and* drive desired business results.

The Critical Need for Change Management

If you ask a typical sales compensation professional to describe the requirements of the job, the list will usually include these things:

- Create sales compensation plans that support the company strategy and motivate the sales force
- Model compensation plans to understand payout and budget expectations
- Create communication materials to support plan rollout

Some people might also include training the sales force on the compensation plan (if not handled by a separate training group) and answering questions from the sales force about the plan design (if not handled by a separate administration team). But even when sales comp professionals include these things, the time spent on training and communication is usually low.

In the vast majority of organizations, more than 80 percent of the incentive plan timeline is devoted to the development of the plan, leaving less than 20 percent of the time to roll it out (see Figure 6-1). In more concrete terms, most organizations will budget around two to three months from start to finish for a new compensation plan design process. Assuming a 12-week timeline, this means that 10 weeks will be spent on strategy development, data collection, plan designs, and plan modeling—and only two weeks will be spent developing the communication and training documents needed to roll out the plan to the sales force.

As discussed in Chapter 3, one of the fundamental purposes of sales compensation professionals is to motivate the sales force to act in a way that supports and drives business goals. While the structure of the sales compensation plan is an important part of

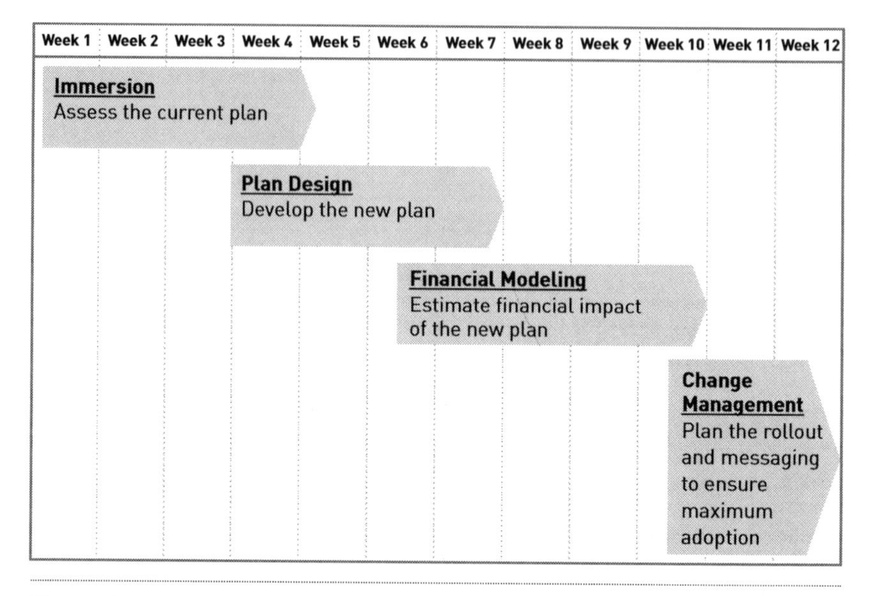

Figure 6-1. *Typical sales incentive plan timeline*

motivation, best-in-class companies in the future will spend as much time ensuring that the sales force understands and believes in the plan as they spend on designing the plan. → IS HOSHIN PLANNING WARRANTED?

Change Management Basics

A widely accepted model of change explains the emotional stages through which people progress when dealing with change (this model is very similar to the stages of grief developed by psychologist Elisabeth Kübler-Ross). The critical emotional stages are:

- Shock
- Anger
- Depression
- Acceptance

These emotions occur when a change is perceived as neutral or negative rather than when it is positive. For example, it's not likely that an excited 18-year-old who was accepted into Harvard is going to experience denial or anger. But an employee who is relocated to a new office, having to leave family and friends behind, may experience these emotions very strongly. When it comes to sales compensation, changes to the comp plan are rarely rolled out to universal acceptance. In some cases, a subset of the sales force is happy with the change—perhaps those who feel disadvantaged by the current design—while in other cases, changes are met with universal resistance (for example, when a company tries to scale back a highly leveraged and very lucrative plan).

When a company changes some aspect of salespeople's work—the sales strategy, the job itself, the products they carry, their manager, or their compensation plan—and that change is not immediately seen in a positive light, we can expect salespeople to go through these different emotional stages. Consider an announcement that the compensation plan will be updated. "We are moving from a commission-based plan," the sales leader announces, "to a goal-based plan. This will equalize earnings opportunities because now everyone will be asked to deliver a number that is based on the potential in your territory. This makes the plan fairer and helps ensure everyone has a realistic objective."

How might top-performing salespeople feel after hearing this announcement? Based on the change management model, they may first feel shock, disbelieving the company would actually make the change. "They're not going to do this," they might say. "No way! I built my territory from scratch!" After some time passes and the reps realize the change is going to happen, the next reaction is anger or blame. "Really!? I can't believe they're going through with this. Whose idea was this? Do they even know anything about sales comp?" It is during this stage that many change initiatives fail: a few vocal detractors who carry influence in the organization oppose the change and cause support to waver. But for organizations that implement the updated plan, the opponents then experience depression. "What's going to happen to me?" they might ask. Eventually, the salespeople move on to acceptance of the change (and adopt new behaviors as a result), and the new paradigm begins to take hold—or they may be so disillusioned that they leave the company.

One of the issues with the rollout of plans in many organizations today is that while comp leaders recognize the anger and uncertainty, little is done to reduce or prevent it. Instead, they often assume that with the appropriate communication and training, the salespeople will—on their own—come to accept the change.

The stages of emotions experienced during a change can be visualized as shown in Figure 6-2. Of course, not all plan changes are significant enough to generate this kind of reaction from the field. Small changes to the plan (for example, a small commission rate adjustment with no change to the metrics or the weights), or changes that are generally well received, may have a shallower "trough" than shown in the diagram.

For big changes (new metrics, changes in strategy, etc.), the change management portion of the plan design process is at least as important as the changes themselves. Our goal as sales compensation professionals in rolling out new plans is to reduce the depth and length of the trough in which salespeople are experiencing negative feelings toward the changes and may be actively fighting them. We need people to accept the change more quickly and act

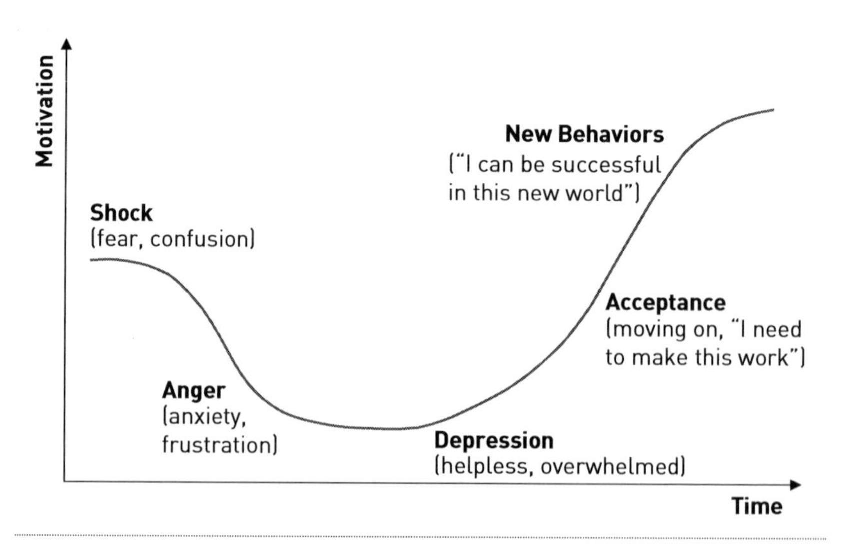

Figure 6-2. *The stages of emotions experienced by a sales force during a change*

Adapted from the work of Elisabeth Kübler-Ross.

on it. Limiting the impact of time spent with decreased levels of motivation will have real financial benefits for companies.

Companies can also combine the concepts in this chapter with concepts in Chapter 5 to go even further with the plan rollout. Chapter 5 provided some ideas for applying predictive analytics to the sales force—specifically, who is likely to call in with questions (or complain) and who is likely to quit. Sales Operations could track rollouts over time to determine which types of salespeople are most likely to have questions and proactively reach out to these people during the rollout phase.

Rolling Out the Plan

When you hear the term "plan rollout," what do you think? For many people today, it means summarizing the plan, creating PowerPoint or Brainshark presentations, and having a couple of meetings with the sales force to explain the new plan metrics and measures. In the future, the communication and change management of the plan will no longer be a stand-alone phase that can be handled at the end of the design process once the plan design details have been finalized. Rather, the communication and change management of the plan will be discussed in every design team meeting, starting with the kickoff meeting. While details of the plan may not be known at the start of the plan design cycle, the sales compensation team must think through how the plan will be rolled out to the field. By keeping their eye on the ultimate goal—motivating salespeople to act—the plan design and ultimately the communication will be much better for it.

How can compensation practitioners maximize the buy-in, understanding, and effectiveness of a reasonably big plan change? In the future, many more companies will likely incorporate the best practices that are done in a few organizations today.

Put Yourself in the Plan Participants' Shoes

While you may have spent the last several months doing a deep dive into the current compensation plan and considering new plan options, the sales team has been doing their daily selling work.

When sales reps see the new plan for the first time, they are starting from scratch—they know nothing about the redesign work that has been done to date. You have to walk them through the process you went through yourself (here is our sales strategy, the data showed this, people said that) to best communicate with them. Empathizing with the salespeople allows comp designers to think through potential issue areas and concerns—hot-button topics that can then be addressed proactively.

One issue often faced by organizations is that salespeople don't trust what Headquarters says. At many organizations, a change in compensation is immediately translated to "They've found a way to pay me less" or "They're going to make me work harder to earn the same amount." It's critically important for the company to understand the salesperson's perspective and to craft the communication accordingly.

Leverage First-Line Managers

Many salespeople work from home and have minimal or no regular daily interaction with other company employees. There are no hallway conversations, water cooler chats, or team meetings with many of their colleagues in a single place. Therefore, the first-line manager is the salesperson's primary connection to the company. When Headquarters shows up with a change to the sales incentive plan, reps look to their first-line managers (and perhaps their peers) to understand whether the change is good for them. First-line managers should always play a critical role in the rollout of the plan, sitting down with their salespeople in one-on-one sessions to talk through what the plan means for them.

Create Rep Advisory Boards

Many organizations have rep "advisory boards" that consist of 6 to 12 talented, high-performing, and well-respected salespeople who are considered "key opinion leaders" in the field. These boards get together on a regular basis (perhaps quarterly) to provide feedback to sales leadership and to be a sounding board for changes that leaders are considering. These advisory boards can be highly useful in the change management process. They should be involved on the front end of the design process, providing input about what's working and what's not working. More important, people in this role can play a critical part in rolling out the new plans to the sales field. Including them in the communication of the plan, given their level of respect and credibility from their peers, will go a long way toward getting salespeople to adopt the new plan and to believe that it is in their best interest as much as it is in the company's.

Three Important Considerations

Communicating about sales compensation can be more challenging than perhaps other corporate communication messages. Sales compensation is how the sales force makes anywhere from 15 percent to more than 70 percent of its pay. Any change affecting a significant portion of an employee's pay is bound to be met with resistance.

As you roll out the plan to the sales force, consider what you want your salespeople to (1) *know*, (2) *do*, and (3) *feel* when they see the new incentive plan. Too often companies focus heavily on the *know* aspect, trust that the *do* aspect will follow, and don't even consider how they want salespeople to *feel*.

1. What They Should Know

It is important that salespeople know how the new incentive plan works, but this knowledge does not support the ultimate objective outlined earlier in the chapter—motivating salespeople to do those things that are in the best interests of the company and themselves. Of course, salespeople must know how the plan works, and that is the foundation for the other elements. Plan rollouts and plan documentation must provide detailed examples of how incentives are calculated under multiple scenarios.

2. What They Should Do

But just knowing how the plan works does not guarantee that salespeople will, or will know how to, do what is necessary to win within the new plan design. In the rollout process, give detailed examples not just of how calculations are done, but of what salespeople in specific situations can do to earn significant incentives. For example, if you are changing the definition of high performer (at least as it relates to high incentive payouts), show a detailed, realistic example of how someone who is in the top 10 percent of earners today could change to move into the top 10 percent of earners under the new plan design. Explain how average performers must shift what they sell, how they sell, how they bundle, and so on, to show exactly how salespeople can maximize their incentive plan. Leave nothing to the imagination.

3. What They Should Feel

Change management requires that comp leaders think through what they want salespeople to *feel* as well as *know* and *do*. For example, a typical sales incentive plan rollout goal may be to ensure that all salespeople can explain the plan to their boss. But if the company considers how they want the salespeople to feel at the end of the rollout process, what would they say?

Perhaps the company wants salespeople to feel excited about the new strategic direction of the organization—that senior leadership understands what it takes to win in the market. Leaders may want the sales force to feel confident that the plan design changes were well thought through and that sales reps are being treated fairly by the company. Management may want the sales force to feel optimistic that they have been given a quota and a set of accounts that makes reaching that quota realistic. Leaders may want the sales force to feel hungry—that the upside in the plan is very lucrative and very reachable. Or perhaps they want reps to trust the company and believe that the sales role is the most important role in the company. You get the idea.

At a minimum, companies should consider the "theme" with which they develop their incentive rollout documentation. Companies that want their salespeople to feel challenged and the desire to achieve may choose a sports-themed rollout. Pictures of mountain climbers summiting or marathoners running across the finish line will elicit a very specific feeling of accomplishment.

Or companies may want their salespeople to feel that they are part of a greater cause than just "selling." Healthcare companies, for example, may want their salespeople to feel like they're part of a team that is changing the industry and improving people's lives. A large cardiology products company achieves this by bringing in patients each year to speak to the company and describe the impact the products have had on their lives and the lives of their loved ones. The stories are moving, and there is not a dry eye in the house. People leave this session reminded of why they work for this company. They also leave with a new awareness of their greater purpose. While this session is not specifically related to sales compensation, the company sends a lot of its sales force to the meeting, and they depart knowing their job is not merely to sell but to save and extend lives.

Rollout Documentation

When developing plan documentation to communicate to the sales force, best-in-class companies will consider these strategies:

1. Don't make the communication too complex. Treat the incentive plan documentation as a marketing brochure, not an engineering diagram. Remember that your ultimate objective is to move the sales force to act, and "simple" will be easier to follow.
2. Don't make it an "overly legalized" document. Some incentive plan documents put all of the legal language up front, essentially telling the salespeople, "Let us tell you why we're not actually going to pay you what is stated later in the document." Needless to say, this type of document is not effective with the sales force and will largely be unread. Legal language is important, but minimize it as much as possible, and put it at the end or in a separate document that can be accessed on the company intranet.
3. Use stories and examples as much as possible. Show what salespeople need to do to change their behavior or selling activities to successfully win in the new plan. Show a realistic example of how someone can change how they approach customers and what the impact would be to their incentive payout. If there

is a real-life example within the sales force demonstrating how a rep has been successful, that's even better.

Once the plan has been rolled out, the responsibilities related to change management are not over. Best-in-class companies will do several things to ensure that the communication of the incentive plan is not "one and done." One example is to include a town hall–style phone Q&A once salespeople have received their first paycheck. Even if they understood the plan the day it was rolled out, the real questions arise when the plan begins affecting their pocketbooks. Another tactic is to provide plan reminders in whatever system your salespeople are likely to access every day—most likely the customer relationship management system or the company's intranet. Provide tips, stories, examples, and so on, showing how the plan has worked for other salespeople in the organization.

Looking Ahead

In the future, best-in-class companies will no longer treat incentive compensation plan rollouts as the last and least difficult phase of a sales incentive plan. They will begin talking about change management and plan communication during the design kickoff meeting (AKA Day 1).

This chapter is not a comprehensive treatise on change management. Entire books have been written on the subject, and several change management models and frameworks can give you a more comprehensive process for rolling out the plan. (If you're interested, look up William Bridges's Transition Model, Kotter International's Eight-Step Process for Leading Change, or McKinsey's 7-S Framework.)

It is our hope that this chapter got you thinking about the enhanced importance of change management when rolling the plan out to the field. Because of the unique nature of the sales role (isolation in the field, autonomous, and so on), leading companies should spend more time on the change management aspect of major plan designs, ensuring that the plan is adopted and understood and that it motivates salespeople to act.

CONCLUSION

~

My interest is in the future because I am going to spend the rest of my life there.

Charles F. Kettering

~

Watch an old science fiction movie that presents itself in a not-so-distant future whose time has come or is about to come (for example, *2001: A Space Odyssey*, *Minority Report*, *Short Circuit*, or *Back to the Future*). In some cases, the predictions are almost comical or incredibly shortsighted. Flying cars are a favorite for reasons that are hard to understand, given our relative difficulty in driving in two dimensions, much less three. Data storage devices look like compact discs, only . . . a little smaller. People travel using matter transportation devices. Other ideas presented in sci-fi movies do not seem so far-fetched, and some of the technologies either have come to fruition or are starting to become reality: artificial intelligence (well, we had to start somewhere, Siri), self-driving cars, and holographic (or virtual reality) communications.

This ability to look back in time, knowing what we know now, makes our retrospective view fun. When we look back on such prognosticating movies, we either marvel at the foresight of the writers or laugh at their naïveté ("People actually thought *that* was going to happen? Ha!").

In general, sci-fi writers ground their assumptions in some measure of reality. Perhaps their inspiration comes from the writing of a futurist or the research of a team of physicists. But rarely are these sci-fi writers simply "making things up." Consider *Star Trek*, the franchise that started as a poorly received TV show in the 1960s and then developed into a cult classic that spawned several generations of movies and TV series. Throughout the various evolutions of *Star Trek*, "Trekkies" and scientists alike debated the merits and feasibility of the technology and the possible future hundreds of years ahead of us. Entire books have been written on this topic, and many of the technologies and much of the science in the show are proving to be feasible. In fact, one of the earliest mobile phones, the Motorola StarTAC, was named because of its likeness to the "communicator" from the original *Star Trek* series.

Much like the writers of *Star Trek* and its various derivatives, we wrote this book with an eye toward the future and what's possible. And although we didn't rely on theoretical science to shape our vision, we leveraged our experiences with our clients, trends in technology, research, thought leadership in our firm, and our own perspectives. Of course, our time horizon is five years, not hundreds of years, into the future.

Perhaps people will read this book 10 years from now (we can hope) and say, "Wow. Chad and Steve were spot-on. They hit the mark on their predictions!" As with any crystal ball gazing, however, it would also not surprise us if some of these predictions end up being inaccurate (although we hope not).

Regardless of the relative accuracy of our predictions, we can state one thing with confidence: sales compensation is not going away.

But, as certain as we are of that fact, we are also equally certain that, like just about anything in life, sales compensation will evolve—and the rate of change is accelerating. The sales compensation programs of tomorrow will no more resemble the sales compensation plans of today than today's salespeople resemble those of early door-to-door salesmen.

In this book, we've touched on a number of subject areas where we believe sales compensation will evolve. Since each subject (and, therefore, each chapter) could be considered in isolation, independently none may seem radically different from current initiatives. However, when you consider all of the chapters holistically, a substantial paradigm shift becomes evident. Sales compensation today is often discussed only in the context of variable pay and sales contests. Sales compensation teams of today are usually built around functions: designing plans, setting quotas, and communicating with the sales force. But imagine for a minute what a "sales compensation" department might look like in the future.

The group would be responsible for developing incentive mechanisms that leverage both intrinsic and extrinsic rewards. Team members will understand that to best motivate and engage the sales force, cash alone may not drive the optimal outcome. Rather, they will know and consider how best to combine elements of both reward mechanisms.

Perhaps this team will also be tasked with studying new research on incentives or behavioral economics, with the goal of creating incentive programs to help both the organization and the salesperson succeed. To support decisions made regarding effective plan designs, this group will be armed with empirical evidence that describes how many metrics should be used or how leveraged the payout curve should be.

The compensation team of the future will also design plans differently. Yes, the fundamental principles of good plan design—fairness, pay-for-performance, alignment with strategic objectives, and so on—will still be required. But this team will also be tasked with collecting information from the sales force to help in this process. Surveys and studies will help practitioners identify the composition and reward preferences of their salespeople. From that information, they will develop incentive strategies that motivate and inspire the sales force to higher performance. The outcome from these studies and investigations can help identify various tactics to improve performance: monetary rewards (if the sales force consists of people who have a strong drive to acquire wealth); nonmonetary incentive vehicles (if the sales force is motivated by other inducements); increasing levels of autonomy and skill development; gamification to drive behavioral change in fun and creative ways; and/or the ability for salespeople to select their own incentive vehicles through "Pick Your Own Plan" options.

As the plan design—no longer a simple sales compensation plan but a more holistic incentive plan—is developed, this group of future practitioners will be thinking of change management throughout the entire process, from the very beginning through the rollout. They will ask, "How can we minimize disruption in the sales force? What can we do to make the incentive rollout as smooth as possible? How can we get salespeople excited about delivering on the sales strategy and goals?" Key stakeholders will be engaged and involved from the start, change champions identified, and communications developed with the salesperson in mind.

Once the incentive plan is rolled out to the sales force, incentive team members will use predictive analytics to continuously monitor and track performance. They will be tasked with predicting possible outcomes much earlier than before and will use data to develop strategies to address those outcomes.

Of course, technology will continue to evolve to facilitate several of this team's functions. Automation will enable incentive practitioners to focus on strategic functions, leaving most of the tactical and manual processes of today to the computer. Technology will also provide large amounts of data and insights that will both aid in the incentive design process and allow for predictive analytics.

Some sales compensation practitioners today may read these predictions and say, "We are already on that path," which may be true on one or more of these dimensions. Other practitioners may read these predictions and see a radical change from their current processes and job responsibilities. For those already on the path, congratulations! For those who feel they are "behind the curve," consider that there is no single right answer. Just as there is no perfect compensation plan, there is no single right amount of change from today.

But as sales compensation practitioners, do we really need to change? As we discussed in Chapter 6, change is hard, so it would not surprise us to hear stories of resistance. This book, however, is not about change for the sake of change. It is about changes that will help both the organization and the salespeople succeed by creating a mutually beneficial situation, one in which both parties get a desired outcome (meaningful incentives for the individual, increased sales for the organization).

In Chapter 3, we discussed four common purposes of a sales compensation program: to attract and retain top salespeople, to motivate (the cliché "What gets you out of bed in the morning?" is appropriate here), to direct behaviors, and to pay for performance. Consider these four elements in today's incentive (or sales compensation) programs. Companies used to offer sales incentives and monetary rewards to hire or poach employees (think Kodak versus Xerox, from Chapter 1). Even today, many organizations get into an "arms race" when it comes to compensation levels. We sometimes hear from companies wondering whether they should increase their pay levels to match a competitor. In one specific case, an organization was trying to attract salespeople for a new sales force, to promote a soon-to-be-released product. To do this, the company believed that the best recruits would come from competitors who already had similar products in the market. It also believed that the way to "poach" these employees was through the incentive program, which would be communicated in advance and effective during the first year of employment. The proposed incentive structure paid a base salary, offered a substantial incentive target with high leverage, and included a lucrative contest (with a payout value equivalent to the incentive target). Motivation, in this example and in many incentive programs of today, is often assumed to be driven by the reward mechanisms: monetary rewards, prizes, contests, and recognition programs. When changing compensation plans, some organizations will comment that they "need to keep the reps motivated" and that any decrease in payout levels is considered unacceptable. Directing behavior is often done implicitly through plan components (essentially telling reps, "You will get paid if you focus on Products A and B," for example). And finally, pay-for-performance describes the fundamental reward mechanism—money (pay)—used to differentiate stars from laggards.

How would (or could) these same four common purposes change in the future?

Companies could use a variety of different techniques to attract and retain salespeople. They could provide a work environment that fosters greater intrinsic motivation and rewards, or they could offer elements of choice. The key is that by designing incentive programs that appeal to their particular sales reps and that reinforce the culture of the organization (or sales teams), companies can move from an "arms race" mentality to one that provides a unique value proposition to their salespeople. Companies in the future may choose to use a "Pick Your Own Plan" approach to maximize motivation. They may use field managers and principles of behavioral economics to help shape and deliver the message to the salespeople. Organizations may further use gamification to shift behaviors in a nonintrusive manner. And finally, pay-for-performance may be replaced by incentives-for-performance, as organizations offer more than monetary rewards for success. In the future, salespeople may have "time off for performance" or "educational credits for performance," if that is what they value.

As you can see, this is a more radical shift when considered holistically. Sales compensation is still a critical part of this program, but current tools and processes (and perhaps even thinking or skills) would need to be updated for this to work. But we believe that these future predictions will come to pass—probably not all at once, but gradually, as companies pilot or deploy solutions that include or implement a subset of these changes.

And if we're wrong? Well, we can always look back and laugh at our sales compensation equivalent of the flying car.

References

Adamson, Brent, Matthew Dixon, and Nicholas Toman. "The End of Solution Sales." *Harvard Business Review*, July–August 2012. https://hbr.org/2012/07/the-end-of-solution-sales.

Akerlof, George A. "The Market for 'Lemons': Quality Uncertainty and the Market Mechanism." *Quarterly Journal of Economics* 84 (August 1970): 488–500.

"As College Graduates Hit the Workforce, So Do More Entitlement-Minded Workers." Press release, University of New Hampshire Media Relations, May 17, 2010. http://www.unh.edu/news/cj_nr/2010/may/lw17gen-y.cfm.

"Book: HP Piloted Program to Predict Which Workers Would Quit." Review of *Predictive Analytics: The Power to Predict Who Will Click, Buy, Lie, or Die. Wall Street Journal*, March 14, 2013.

Bridges, William, and Susan Bridges. *Managing Transitions: Making the Most of Change*. Boston: Da Capo Press, 2009.

Brosnan, Sarah F., and Frans B. M. de Waal. "Monkeys Reject Unequal Pay." *Nature* 425 (September 18, 2003): 297–99.

Bryan, Lowell. "Enduring Ideas: The 7-S Framework." *McKinsey Quarterly*, March 2008. http://www.mckinsey.com/insights/strategy/enduring_ideas_the_7-s_framework.

Camerer, Colin F., George Loewenstein, and Matthew Rabin. *Advances in Behavioral Economics*. The Roundtable Series in Behavioral Economics. Princeton, NJ: Princeton University Press, 2003.

Condly, Steven J., Richard E. Clark, and Harold D. Stolovitch. "The Effects of Incentives on Workplace Performance: A Meta-analytic Review of Research Studies." *Performance Improvement Quarterly* 16, no. 3 (2003): 46–63.

Deming, W. Edwards. *Out of the Crisis*. Cambridge, MA: MIT Press, 2000.

Doug, J., Thomas Steenburgh, and K. Sudhir. "Do Bonuses Enhance Sales Productivity? A Dynamic Structural Analysis of Bonus-Based Compensation Plans." Harvard Business School, Boston, MA, 2010. http://www.hbs.edu/faculty/Publication%20Files/11-041_078c27e5-110c-4029-8576-108139a05b77.pdf.

"Employee Tenure Summary." U.S. Bureau of Labor Statistics, U.S. Department of Labor, September 18, 2014. http://www.bls.gov/news.release/tenure.nr0.htm.

Fry, Richard. "This Year, Millennials Will Overtake Baby Boomers." Pew Research Center, January 16, 2015. http://www.pewresearch.org/fact-tank/2015/01/16/this-year-millennials-will-overtake-baby-boomers.

Gartner Methodologies. "Gartner Hype Cycle." N.d. http://www.gartner.com/technology/research/methodologies/hype-cycle.jsp.

Holmes, Pete. "Google (Not Knowing)." YouTube, March 29, 2011. https://www.youtube.com/watch?v=PQ4o1N4ksyQ.

Jenkins, G. Douglas, Jr., Atul Mitra, Nina Gupta, and Jason D. Shaw. "Are Financial Incentives Related to Performance? A Meta-analytical Review of Empirical Research." *Journal of Applied Psychology* 83, no. 5 (September 1998): 777–87.

Kotter International. "The 8-Step Process for Leading Change." N.d. http://www.kotterinternational.com/the-8-step-process-for-leading-change.

Kübler-Ross, Elisabeth. *On Grief and Grieving: Finding the Meaning of Grief Through the Five Stages of Loss*. New York: Scribner, 2007.

Lawrence, Paul R., and Nitin Nohria. *Driven: How Human Nature Shapes Our Choices*. San Francisco: Jossey-Bass, 2002.

Lawrence, Paul, and Nitin Nohria. "Driven: How Human Nature Shapes Organizations." Harvard Business School Working Knowledge, Boston, MA, October 9, 2001. http://hbswk.hbs.edu/item/driven-how-human-nature-shapes-organizations.

Maslow, Abraham. "A Theory of Human Motivation." *Psychological Review* 50 (1943): 370–96.

McGonigal, Jane. *Reality Is Broken: Why Games Make Us Better and How They Can Change the World*. New York: Penguin, 2011.

McGregor, Jena. "Is Google Squeezing Its '20% Time'?" *Business Week*, June 6, 2008. http://www.businessweek.com/careers/managementiq/archives/2008/06/is_google_squee.html.

Moore, Brian. "The Worst Generation?" *New York Post*, May 10, 2010. http://nypost.com/2010/05/10/the-worst-generation/#ixzz0pNJCGGAD.

Palca, Joe. "Monkey Business: Fairness Isn't Just a Human Trait." *NPR*, August 18, 2010. http://www.npr.org/templates/story/story.php?storyId=129233715.

Pettypiece, Shannon. "Unintended Consequence of Wal-Mart's Raise: Unhappy Workers." *BloombergBusiness*, August 6, 2015. http://www.bloomberg.com/news/articles/2015-08-06/an-unintended-consequence-of-wal-mart-pay-raise-unhappy-workers?cmpid=yhoo.

Pink, Daniel H. *Drive: The Surprising Truth About What Motivates Us*. New York: Riverhead Books, 2011.

Sahad, Jeanne. "Guess Which Huge Company Now Offers Unlimited Vacation." July 13, 2015. http://money.cnn.com/2015/07/13/pf/general-electric-unlimited-paid-time-off/.

Schuster, Mike. "'Instant Everything' Has Turned Us into Jerks." *Minyanville*, March 23, 2012. http://www.minyanville.com/mvpremium/2012/03/23/instant-everything-has-turned-us.

Siegel, Eric, and Thomas H. Davenport. *Predictive Analytics: The Power to Predict Who Will Click, Buy, Lie, or Die*. Hoboken, NJ: Wiley & Sons, 2013.

Silverman, Rachel Emma, and Nikki Waller. "The Algorithm That Tells the Boss Who Might Quit." *Wall Street Journal*, March 13, 2015. http://www.wsj.com/articles/the-algorithm-that-tells-the-boss-who-might-quit-1426287935.

Society for Human Resource Management. "Employee Job Satisfaction and Engagement: The Road to Economic Recovery." N.d. http://www.shrm.org/Research/SurveyFindings/Documents/14-0028%20JobSatEngage_Report_FULL_FNL.pdf.

Sosna, Erica. "The Importance of Narrative." BlessingWhite, August 2014. http://blessingwhite.com/article/2014/08/19/the-importance-of-narrative.

Steenburgh, Thomas, and Michael Ahearne. "Motivate Your Core Performers to Become Star Performers." *Harvard Business Review*, August 3, 2012. https://hbr.org/2012/08/incentivize-your-core-performe.

——. "Motivating Sales People: What Really Works." Presentation for the Sales Force Productivity Conference, Atlanta, GA, October 23–25, 2012.

——. "Motivating Salespeople: What Really Works." *Harvard Business Review*, July–August 2012. https://hbr.org/2012/07/motivating-salespeople-what-really-works.

Tversky, Amos, and Daniel Kahneman. "The Framing of Decisions and the Psychology of Choice." *Science* 211, no. 4481 (January 30, 1981): 453–58.

Twenge, Jean M., Stacy M. Campbell, Brian J. Hoffman, and Charles E. Lance. "Generational Differences in Work Values: Leisure and Extrinsic Values Increasing, Social and Intrinsic Values Decreasing." *Journal of Management* 36, no. 5 (September 2010): 1117–42. doi: 10.1177/0149206309352246.

"2014 National Population Projections." U.S. Census Bureau, U.S. Department of Commerce, n.d. http://www.census.gov/population/projections/data/national/2014.html.

Vroom, Victor H. *Work and Motivation*. San Francisco: Jossey-Bass, 1994.

Weise, Karen. "A Lie Detector Test for Online Reviewers." *BloombergBusiness*, September 29, 2011. http://www.bloomberg.com/bw/magazine/a-lie-detector-test-for-online-reviewers-09292011.html.

Wiersma, Uco J. "The Effects of Extrinsic Rewards in Intrinsic Motivation: A Meta-analysis." *Journal of Occupational and Organizational Psychology* 65, no. 2 (June 1992): 101–14. doi: 10.1111/j.2044-8325.1992.tb00488.x.

Zoltners, Andris A., Prabhakant Sinha, and Sally E. Lorimer. *The Complete Guide to Sales Force Incentive Compensation: How to Design and Implement Plans That Work*. New York: AMACOM, 2006.

Acknowledgments

As consultants, we have worked personally with executives, sales leaders, sales managers, and salespeople at hundreds of companies all over the world. Collectively, our work has included designing more than 1,000 different sales comp plans for more than 250 companies. The clients of ZS have helped us discover, cultivate, test, and refine many of the concepts described in this book. Because of confidentiality, many of the people and companies must remain anonymous, but we owe a great deal of gratitude to all those who have helped us develop and enhance our ideas over the years. Special contributions to this book came from Brian Sinclair, Mike Rutz, Doug Brown, Marc Schoenen, Justin Ford, Steve Herz, Doug Smith, Sherra Buckley and the GoalQuest team, Chris Cabrera, Evan Ellis, and Jay Graves.

We would especially like to thank Andy Zoltners, co-founder of ZS, for writing the foreword to the book and collaborating with us to solve sales compensation issues for more than a decade. Andy has always challenged us to think differently, question the status quo, and innovate. His mentoring drove us to look ahead and not rely on what we have done in the past. His quest for innovation and high performance has compelled us to do the same.

In addition, many colleagues at ZS contributed to the book directly and indirectly, including Steve Redden and Brian Thompson, who both helped review the manuscript and suggest enhancements for clarity. Lisa Davis led the book's production and editorial efforts, reviewing the manuscript multiple times, and keeping us on track to meet every publishing deadline. Sally Lorimer edited the foreword as well as other portions of the book.

We would also like to thank ZS publishing partner Books By Design, including Nancy Benjamin and Carol Keller, and the ZS marketing team, including Aaron Smith and Laurie Mahoney, who assisted with the book's marketing plans, and Neil Warner, Melanie McKnight, Purnendu Chakraborty, and Ganesh Singh, who designed the book's covers, page layouts, and graphics.

Without the efforts of these hardworking collaborators, this book would not be in your hands today.

Chad Albrecht

Steve Marley

Index

You may be interested in the following books written by leaders at ZS.

The Power of Sales Analytics
Discover how to use analytics, data, and technology to improve fundamental sales force decisions and create competitive advantage. Included is a blueprint for creating the organizational capabilities sales leaders need to cost-effectively put analytics to work by assembling the right combination of internal and external resources.

Building a Winning Sales Management Team
Written with input from 19 successful sales executives from leading companies, this book focuses on the pivotal role of the first-line sales manager as a force behind the sales force and a critical link between salespeople, customers, and the company. Discover how by investing in the sales management team, companies can drive profitable growth in an ever-changing business environment.

Building a Winning Sales Force
Master a proven framework for assessing how good a sales force is and finding ways to improve it through better decisions about key sales effectiveness drivers, such as sales force design, hiring, training, incentive compensation, and performance management. The authors also address many challenging issues, including how to implement sales strategy changes, allocate sales resources, and retain successful salespeople.

The Complete Guide to Sales Force Incentive Compensation
This detailed guide is packed with hundreds of real-life examples of what works and what doesn't when it comes to creating a sales incentive compensation program that drives results, including how to design and implement a program that aligns with your company's goals and culture, while avoiding the common trap of overusing incentives to solve too many sales management problems.

Coming in 2017

Current Issues in Sales Incentive Compensation
Learn about the top challenges faced by sales compensation professionals today, along with practical suggestions for addressing them. The authors discuss the impact of technology on sales incentives, how to design plans that drive profitability, and how to design effective global plans, among other challenges.